FINDI[ ]
FABULOUS
OVER 60

OVERCOMING
TRAUMA AND ADDICTION

WEIGHT LOSS THAT
FINALLY WORKED

DETACHING FROM A
NIGHTMARE RELATIONSHIP

LESLEY THOMAS

First published by Ultimate World Publishing 2020
Copyright © 2020 Lesley Thomas

ISBN

Paperback: 978-1-922497-54-3
Ebook: 978-1-922497-55-0

Cover design: Ultimate World Publishing
Layout and typesetting: Ultimate World Publishing
Editor: Emily Riches

Ultimate World Publishing
Diamond Creek,
Victoria Australia 3089
www.writeabook.com.au

Testimonials

"*Finding Fabulous Over 60* is a very open, honest and raw account of Lesley's colourful journey through life. She openly shares her experiences of trauma and addiction, relationship and weight challenges and how her recovery and healing led her to a life of thriving, wellness and inner peace. This book will give hope to many and a realisation that anything is possible!"

Sue Stone, UK Author, Secret Millionaire and Inspirational Speaker (Author of *Love Life Live Life* and *The Power Within You Now*)

"Lesley Thomas has been on a journey of self-discovery for many years and has attended many event productions worldwide with an array of the most thought-provoking teachers in the self-help industry. Her knowledge of the human condition, and herself, has inspired her to share with the world years of dedicated learning and development. She is genuine and loving. I am so thrilled that the world will benefit from her courage in sharing her experiences and journey with us all!"

Ibis Kaba, Exec. VP/Producer – Life Journeys, Inc.

"Lesley Thomas' book is real, it's raw, it's gutsy, it's transformational. She takes you on an often-perilous journey from challenging and chaotic, to a sense of calm and easeful living. This is her experience and she IS fabulous and over 60. I recommend this book. You will laugh and cry, and you never know... you may also transform."

Chris Hooper, Chris Hooper Promotions
Since 1972 – Events for heart • soul • body • mind
Tour Producers, Event Creators & Managers
& Event Organisers

"This book represents one woman's struggle to examine and make meaning of her life. Lesley lays open the 'bare bones' of her experiences in a bitingly honest stream of consciousness. This personal journey is entertaining as well as poignant and has inspiration for others also wishing to shed light on their own stories."

Lucy Brooks, BSc Psych/Ed; Post Grad Dip. Psych
Counselling (University of Surrey, UK)

"Lesley's book is very moving. Spoken from the heart, a real life story. Easy to read (for both men and women), it's therapeutic, genuine and completely engaging."

Diane Smith, formerly of
Breast Cancer Care Western Australia

"Lesley's thought provoking and brutally honest account of the dilemmas and ultimate insights she has faced in her life gives both clarity and hope for almost every woman who reads it. While it is unlikely that many of us have faced every troubling issue she describes, every woman will identify with at least one of these and take inspiration from it…"

Christine Wells, BA (Soc. Sci.) BA App. Sci. (Speech and Hearing Science)

"This is a memoir of healing. I hope that Lesley's courage in writing and sharing her story will inspire others to wade into what's been holding them back from the life they were meant to live – to take their power and beauty back for good."

Jacob Nordby, Author of *The Creative Cure: How Finding and Freeing Your Inner Artist Can Heal Your Life*

"A touching and personal story about how life talks to you and whether you choose to listen. The words tear away the pretence of what we naively expect in life and replaces it with the strength to face the reality of personal growth. Inspirational and revealing…"

Roderick Davies, Author of Australian Technical History

"Lesley's best qualities are her abilities to listen, to care, to support, to help, to encourage and to be there for you if you needed her. In some of my own darkest days she helped me overcome my fears and restore my strength when I could no longer believe or see a future due to my illness. Lesley has also had to deal with many lows in her life and her positive outlook (even when it was extremely difficult) and her strength to get through it is inspirational."

Dominica Mirabella, Melbourne

Dedication

This book is dedicated to Kelly and Tom and to an incredibly loving Power greater than me that guided me to write this book.

Contents

Introduction

"There is no greater agony than bearing an untold story
inside you."

MAYA ANGELOU

This book is intended for anyone who is struggling to overcome traumas, addictions, yoyo dieting and weight issues or who is wanting to get away from an unhealthy relationship and would appreciate reading about how someone else managed to overcome them.

It is also for women in their 50s, 60s and 70s+ who may think life has passed them by. It hasn't!

I have a beautiful full-length window which my desk sits up against. Early every morning, I sit in my rotating chair with my feet up on a thigh-high stool with a cup of hot coffee in hand and in the quiet and stillness, I watch the sun come slowly over the low rooftops and through the trees. It is such an incredible and magical sight.

1

Every day is different and yet still so stunning. It was here where I talked with a Power greater than me, and felt inspired to write this book. I am not a religious person; I just believe there is something out there more powerful than me, which I choose to call God, and I find when I spend time with that Power, I can be greatly inspired.

Learning of the wonderful gifts of healing I have been blessed with, the reader will hopefully be inspired and motivated to keep going on their own journey or become willing to make their own major changes to achieve similar results.

It came to me one morning in early August 2020 that I was meant to tell my story now and help others with their own mental, emotional, physical and spiritual hurdles to do with addictions, traumas, weight and relationship issues.

CHAPTER ONE

These Carrots are Tasteless

A man I lived with for three years in my early 40s had just taken his first mouthful of what I thought was a delicious evening meal. With a really pissed-off tone, he announced, "these carrots are tasteless." When I asked what was wrong with them, he said they should have been cooked with honey and sugar and he had a condescending "you are so useless" look on his face.

Another night, he told me that the onions in my spaghetti bolognese weren't chopped up small enough. I remember telling a group of women about it a few years ago and one woman said, "OMG! I was with a man who said that to me too, so the next time I made spaghetti bolognese I just cut the onion in half and put it in the pan like that!" I wish I had thought of that at the time.

I was totally "over" the cooking complaints by the time he got to asking, "where is the homemade apple sauce to go with these pork chops"? and "why aren't the pork chops crumbed?" But it was when he turned to me one day and asked why I hadn't darned his socks that I really blew a gasket (or perhaps it was when he gave me an electric hedge cutter for Christmas to save me time cutting all the hedges with the sheers. No, I think it was the time he came into the bathroom while I was in the shower and looked me up and down and said I'd put on weight on my stomach and I'd better lose it, as he didn't want me embarrassing myself in bathers). I remember telling a girl at work about all of this and asking her if she darned her husband's socks. She told me about an event early in her marriage when her husband had brought one of his shirts to her saying there was a button missing. She'd told him "Oh, I don't do buttons." He'd been completely dumbfounded and had wandered off into the distance babbling incoherently. I took that as a "no."

I didn't realise it at the time, but the infernal nitpicking and never-ending putdowns about me or anything and everything I had or had not done were chipping away at my soul and crushing my spirit. Why didn't I leave? Good point, but the problem at the time was that I didn't have much self-esteem, and sometimes he was really nice to me and this would give me hope that things might work out. Plus, there was plenty of my own "stuff" that I was not dealing with. I also found that I was attached to him in some unfathomable way, which I learned many years later was codependency. At the time though, I just couldn't work out why it was so impossible for me to leave. For the first time in my life, I understood why women stayed with men like this.

A point came where I did leave though, which I will talk about later, but once I had left, I knew I had to look at what it was about me that had attracted a man like that in the first place. I had to take responsibility for that. I also had to look at "my part" in our relationship breakdown, as I did not ever, ever want to repeat it. The only way to do that was to address and change whatever I needed to about myself.

And to do that, I needed to start with the unprocessed traumas in my childhood, my addictions, character defects, weight issues, life choices, and obsessive-compulsive behaviour as an adult. This was work I did not want to do, but I knew in my heart that I had to. I would have been far more enthusiastic at the time if I had known in advance the magic in the journey, and that it was possible to process and overcome all of these issues. I wanted to feel wonderful on the inside and be happy and free.

So, in July 1998, aged 44, I started my internal journey with counselors and psychologists to go through all of these things and more. I also read every self-help book I could lay my hands on and I even started going to church for a while. I started with my childhood and looked at our family life at home. I loved my parents very much. There were both really good people and provided all the essentials – food, home, clothing, education, etc. However, my father was incredibly strict and I always felt like I was walking around on eggshells. I know mum and dad loved myself and my two brothers very much, but we were kept at an arm's length, so (to me at least) that love was hardly recognisable. We were to be seen and not heard – but that was the way mum and dad had been brought up, so that's all they knew. You can't teach something you haven't learned yourself, so I can't blame them.

Dad also always looked annoyed – he was a serious man and I'm sure he just didn't realise how he came across. He had a brilliant sense of humour, but we didn't get to see much of it as we were growing up through our primary school years. Mum was always working either in the kitchen, garden, or around the house and she just didn't look happy – to me anyway. Dad worked hard building up a business, as did mum keeping an immaculate home and garden. Mum always served up delicious home-cooked meals; we never had a takeaway. I don't even think takeaway was invented back then.

Mum was a 50s mum and every evening had dad's cheese and biscuits and glass of sherry ready for when he got home from work at exactly 6 pm. Mum would ring a big loud bell outside at 5 pm every day so that wherever we kids were, we could hear it and get straight home to be bathed and in our jarmies by 6 pm. We were not allowed anywhere near dad for a half hour after he got home to give him time to unwind from work and enjoy his drink and nibbles.

Mum made most of our clothes. A few things she instilled in me over and over again from day dot were "there's not enough money for this or that," "don't ever let anyone touch you," and "when you marry, never say no to your husband, he'll just go somewhere else to get it if you do." This instilled in me a belief system of lack and while I had no frigging idea of what "it" was, I was really scared of men.

I remember watching mum putting my younger brother's nappies through the wringer. There was no washing machine in those days and mum didn't have a car either for many, many years. Mum also used to cut all the grass edges with scissors and there were loads of edges.

Every meal was eaten together at a round table and we had to eat everything on our plates or we would be in deep trouble. If we swore, mum would wash out our mouths with soap and water. I'll never forget saying "shit" out loud one day and out came the soap and the taste was just awful. The ridiculous thing was that I expected not to be able to swear again and was quite surprised when I found I easily could. I was always playing in the garden or climbing trees and getting dirty. If my brothers or I were naughty, we would hear mum rattling around in a kitchen drawer looking for a wooden spoon to whack us with or she would call out for me to climb the umbrella tree and get a big stick and would lay right into whoever she had her sights on.

My brothers and I spent a great deal of time in the back garden playing in empty cartons and boxes that dad brought home from his warehouse. We spent many a happy hour making cubbies or building planes. We also had a treehouse that dad made. It was just a large flat platform of wood in the centre of the tree branches, but there was also a thick rope that we could climb up and down on or just have a great swing on. I loved that treehouse and rope.

Dad ran the household like he was still in the navy in wartime. Every morning, I would wake to dad's voice calling out loudly "TTH," which stood for "Toilet, Teeth, Hands" i.e. get up immediately and go to the toilet, brush your teeth and wash your hands. You absolutely wouldn't dream of being disobedient. When dad gave a command, we would instantly obey or all hell would break loose. After our TTH, we had timed hot showers before dad would call out "cold on" where we had to turn all the hot water off and have a freezing cold shower. Dad would come into the bathroom and stick his hand under the shower to make sure we were doing it too. The truly ridiculous thing about that is that I still have a freezing cold shower today after my hot shower. I don't feel fresh without it. Crazy, but it says a lot for the power of instilling belief systems into children for the first seven years of their life!

7

The very best thing that ever happened in my childhood was my parents booking Peacock Cottage on Rottnest Island for two weeks over the Christmas holidays when I was about 11 or 12. I was beside myself with excitement. From then on, for several years, we had two weeks at that cottage each Christmas. Mum and dad were also permitted by the island authority to put up two large permanent tents, one of which mum made herself. We had a great spot away from all the noisy campers in tent land and were also able to go for weekends or school holidays throughout the year and it was just wonderful. Dad was a tiny bit more relaxed, but still controlled our every move on these trips, but during school holidays he would only join us on the weekends, so we had much more freedom during the week with just mum and we loved that.

Next, I looked at the traumas I had experienced in my childhood. In Year 3, at primary school, I had an incredibly humiliating experience. I was seven years old and put my hand up to ask permission to go to the toilet. The teacher said no. Fear completely gripped me, as I didn't just want a wee, I needed to do a poo! Worse, I was wearing my loose undies and I still remember the intense panic I felt knowing that poo was coming out, that it was likely to ooze through the open slats of my chair and land on the floor underneath me and there was absolutely nothing I could do to stop it. I remember looking to my left at a boy across a short aisle. His face said it all – total disbelief and disgust as he glanced from my face to the poo on the floor under me. I immediately started crying and just got up and walked out of the classroom and kept going all the way home. I didn't want to go to school the next day, but my parents made me. I felt like I had no choice and just had to face it. It was so humiliating. A couple of the boys from my class made things worse by bullying me incessantly for the next few years calling me "Cadburys Carmelo." All I wanted to be as a little girl was a fairy princess and I was devastated by this event.

Also aged seven, I had a serious accident. I was home from school and sitting on the back step watching mum practice her golf tee-off swing with a wood club. She was right in front of me and was teeing off to the bottom of the back garden. I got the idea that I could run out just as she hit the tee and quickly find the tee before she finished swinging. I wanted to impress her by my speed in doing that, to get her attention. Unfortunately, when I ran out, I collected the full swing of the club on my left temple, which resulted in me being in and out of hospital for the next 18 months and having four operations.

While in hospital, I had some terrible experiences. I remember so clearly the look on my mum's face just before she turned to leave after I had been screaming out to be allowed to kiss her goodbye. But the hospital staff who had me pinned on a trolley bed wouldn't let her, as they took me off for an operation. Mum had looked really traumatised and I know I certainly was. Tears had filled her eyes as she put her hand up to cover her mouth, turned away, and left; I had a sick-to-my-guts feeling that I would never see her again. Absolute panic filled me. I fought to get free with everything I had. I was desperate to kiss mum goodbye, but I was held down by four nurses. This was a horrible way to go into the operating theatre and there was nothing I could do about it. I just had to suck it up.

Waking up after an operation was a truly frightening experience in those days. It was an extremely slow process and I remember the fear I felt when I was becoming aware but had no control over my body. Once I was more awake, I found myself on a trolley somewhere – in a room or a passageway – and no one was around. I felt so alone, scared, and abandoned.

Another day, my whole left eye area became infected and a huge bag of pus completely covered my left eye. It seemed to be both inside and outside of my eyelid as well as covering the eye itself and was extremely painful. I was taken into a room, a doctor looked at it and then his hand holding a sharp needle slowly descended to my eye. I was terrified and begged for an anaesthetic, screamed for one, but I was completely ignored. They just held me down and stuck the needle in my eye. I had never experienced such excruciating pain and screamed my lungs out. I still remember lying on a bed afterward in Recovery for hours just staring into space. I couldn't even speak I was that shocked by the pain of it. I was terribly upset that these people could do that to me without any regard for how I felt. And my parents weren't there protecting me. I felt completely powerless and I hated it and it made me really, really angry.

Another time, I was given a type of wrap to put on, then was wheeled into a private room. A group of young student doctors came in and surrounded the bed. I was horrified when one of these young doctors opened up the wrap I was wearing and exposed my naked body. I tried to pull the wrap back over me, but he just smirked and pulled it off my crotch area again. I remember feeling humiliated and fearful but have absolutely no recollection of what happened after that. Perhaps nothing; I just don't know.

When I was ten, a serial murderer started terrorising the area where we lived and nearby areas. We lived in Perth, Western Australia in an era when crime was virtually nonexistent. People didn't even lock their front doors. All of a sudden, someone was going around shooting people in the middle of the night and the police had no idea who it was, nor any leads. Also, there was either someone else or the same person running people down in the street and killing them. The police were so desperate to find who was responsible that they even went to people's homes and fingerprinted any male over 12 years of age. Dad and my older brother were both fingerprinted. Everyone was terrified; we even had bars put on all our windows.

None of these things that happened in my childhood were ever talked about again. There certainly wasn't any counseling or trauma services at the time either. I just had to cop it all. I was so fearful by the time I was ten that I had terrible nightmares and wet my bed until I was 15 years old.

I had a huge comfort come into my life during this time though. TV had come to Perth. It was black and white and had one channel. My favourite time of day was after school when I would sit with my afternoon tea and watch TV. I didn't have to think and I could relax, as dad wouldn't be home until 6 pm. If we had a babysitter though, dad would cross off any programs we were not allowed to watch, which really annoyed me.

A wonderful treat was Saturday afternoon at the pictures down the road. Dad would give us two shillings for the movie and three pence for a packet of lifesavers. While gone, mum and dad would have "a rest." If the movies weren't on or if it was a Sunday, we kids had to have a rest on our beds for two hours in the afternoon. The whole house shut down so that mum and dad could have their rest. It wasn't until many years later that mum told me what they were really doing.

One film had a huge impact on me. So much so that at the time I went to see it several times in the city. The film was *Ben-Hur*. It was made in 1959, starring Charlton Heston and it won 11 Academy Awards. I mention it because even as a child and although I wasn't religious, it moved me deeply. Not once in the film did you see Jesus' face, but there were two scenes in which Ben-Hur (Charlton Heston) looked into the eyes of Jesus. To this day, I have never forgotten the expression on Ben-Hur's face, especially the second time. I've always wondered what he saw. Every time over the years that this movie came on TV, I would drop everything and watch it again. Today, I have three copies and usually watch it at least once or twice a year. It is still the greatest movie ever made for me.

We were not well off but rented in a very affluent suburb until I was 13. We were surrounded by wealthy people that lived in beautiful homes and could buy whatever they wanted, whenever they wanted. This instilled in me a huge sense of being "less than." My parents were also constantly telling me what to "be," "do," and "don't do," such as "be sweet, be ladylike…" anything but be me, which was more tomboy and this made me feel that they didn't like who I was, that I was somehow "wrong." Dad also had a habit of bringing out his school report to show me how much better his report was than mine at report time, which further instilled my "not good enough" feelings. My heart would sink as I looked at the floor.

Basically, I felt pretty worthless as a child and was always busting my boiler to get attention or I was off eating food and watching TV. Dad would come crashing down on me with an angry "Lezzie, desist," which would shut me right up if I was saying or doing something he didn't like. I also never had a say in anything: my opinion was not valued, nor wanted. I had no voice growing up. I think that is why I have always gone to great lengths to be heard, understood, and validated in my adult life – to the point of being aggressive about it.

There was one very difficult time when mum thought dad was having an affair with his secretary and was extremely jealous and suspicious of the young woman. Dad wasn't having an affair (the girl was having a relationship with one of the other chaps in the office), but mum had it in her head that he was, and life at home was really tense for some time. In later years, I learned that I had become a surrogate for my mother's feelings. I could feel the intensity of her jealousy and suspicion in my body as a child and it created enormous anxiety for me at the time and came up again in my relationships with men as an adult.

I think mum took her anger over this out on me one day when she got annoyed that my beautiful long blond hair was knotty. Mum always cut my hair, but this time she marched me down to the local hairdresser shop and told them to cut off all my hair right up to my ears all the way around. I was mortified, but I had no choice in the matter.

Dad told me in later years that he thought he had been a mild parent in comparison to his father. He and mum had extremely tough childhoods. How could I blame them for their strictness? Unfortunately, dad kept ordering me around for the rest of his life and I just couldn't stand it. All I wanted to do was get away from him.

So, throughout this start to my internal journey, I was searching for something and I had no idea what. I just wanted to feel better on the inside. Progress was slow because I was drinking and smoking heavily plus I worked full time in a fairly mind-numbing job. Fortunately, the girls I worked with were excellent fun, which was like a balm during that time. I was also experiencing an extremely painful withdrawal from the three-year, codependent, nightmare relationship I had been in, which had left me absolutely reeling.

Next, I needed to look at my teenage and early adult years, as well as the development of my addictions and insanely obsessive compulsive behaviour. I knew that was not going to be easy or pretty.

CHAPTER TWO

Out of Control

My teenage years at MLC (Methodist Ladies' College) were happier than my childhood. I had such a great time with my girlfriends at this school. My nightmares lessened and I stopped wetting my bed finally when I was 15.

One hilarious episode at school happened when my buddykins Gillus and I decided to wag assembly. We thought we'd hide briefly in what we called the time tunnel until everyone had gone down to the big hall. Then we would get out and up to some mischief. The time tunnel was an area level with and off a main outdoor pathway. The opening was about 4 feet high and 6 feet wide, so we had to bend over to get in. It went in about 20 feet under a building. It had concrete walls and ceiling, with sand and rubble on the ground. We waited until all the students had gone past and were about to come out when a teacher stopped and stood right in front of the opening with her back to us. We were right back in the tunnel and could only see her legs. If she had looked in the tunnel, she wouldn't have seen us, as it was quite black after a few feet. At this point, I really, really needed to go to the toilet and do a poo. Memories of my classroom episode as a child came flooding back, but this time it was really funny. Gillus was begging me to hold on, but the teacher wasn't budging, so I had to do it then and there in the sand and rubble. Poor Gillus was keeling over and although I nearly "self" asphyxiated, I was absolutely pissing myself listening to her trying to quietly dry retch.

Another time, Gillus and I decided to wag school for the afternoon. Instead of discreetly slipping out and ducking down a side street, we walked out of the front gate and stood on the other side of the highway opposite the school. We had just started thumbing for a ride when a car stopped. It was Gillus's mum, Dorothy. OMG! Sprung, big time. But she just asked where we were headed and when I said, "my place," she said that's where she was going too and to hop in, she'd give us a lift. We couldn't believe our luck, nor her attitude.

Around this time, we moved from the house we had been renting for ten years into a home my parents bought a few streets away. My mum really came into herself in this new home and was a lot happier. She was a bit older, much more confident and she was able to do a lot more with her gifts in creating a beautiful home and garden in our new home. She also excelled hostessing dinner parties for dad's overseas clients or their friends. She was an incredibly lovely and extremely capable person. Everyone loved my mum. She could do anything she set her mind to. We kids adored her, and she was a wonderful mother in many ways.

Not long after we moved though, she did something completely out of character. She had my cat and its kitten put down because they were wrecking her new garden. I found out when I got home from school and I was devastated. She didn't even talk to me about it first or consider my feelings. Worse, I didn't get to say goodbye to them. This was how both my parents treated us kids when it came to what they wanted. How we felt just didn't come into it at all and I was deeply hurt by this treatment. Again, I just had to suck it up.

Mum and dad entertained a lot. A heck of a lot. They had entertained in our previous home, but it increased after we moved. Dad's business was also doing well and things were not quite so tight financially. I loved their dinner parties. I always had a lot of fun, even if I was just helping mum serve and wash dishes in the kitchen! Apart from losing my precious cats, the years at MLC in this home were the happiest in my life. Until I was 17.

When I was 16, I met my first boyfriend at a school formal dance. I remember being so excited when he asked me out. Dad thought he was ideal because he called him "sir." Unbeknownst to me, before a first date with any young man, dad had him and his family checked out to make sure they were of good breeding. This really infuriated me when I found out about it some years later.

He was a great boyfriend, considerate, well mannered and gorgeous to me. After our first night out, he said he'd call me the next day. When I took the call, dad made sure I had noted that he had turned over the three-minute egg timer. I knew what that meant. I had to be off the phone before the timer ran out. But I wasn't was I, I was still talking. My dad was so enraged by my disobedience that he ripped the phone cord clean out of the wall. I was gobsmacked and I honestly didn't think my new boyfriend would ever call again, but he did.

At 16, I was incredibly naive, extremely modest, and a bit more than scared when it came to intimacy. I also had a huge problem with anyone looking at me naked and always went to great lengths to ensure that none of my family or friends ever caught me undressed. It was several months before my boyfriend and I actually got into bed together. I had had virtually zero sex education up to that point and after we made love for the first time (in pitch-black darkness at my insistence), my boyfriend asked, "did you come?" I had absolutely no frigging idea what he was talking about. It wasn't until several years later when I was woken up during the night by the sound of my roommate masturbating when I was an air hostess that I found out what an orgasm was. My roommate also kindly explained to me a few ways to experience this wonder upon wonders for myself.

When I was 17 and in my final year at MLC, my dad advised me that when I left school I either could go to uni, finishing school in Melbourne, Victoria or if I stayed at home, I had to get a job, provide for myself and pay board to contribute to the household expenses.

I'd been brought up with mum drumming into me that when I grew up I'd get married, have kids and my husband would be the provider. Amazingly, I had never questioned that; I just accepted it and expected it to happen. Before marriage, I wanted to be an air hostess, but in those days the entry age was 21 and you also had to be a qualified nurse to be accepted. So mum took me to meet some people who could advise us on nursing, but I felt very intimidated by these people, and as weird as this sounds, I hated the building they were in. I felt incredibly uncomfortable in it. I think it must have reminded me of the building I was in as a child in hospital. It was also located close to that hospital, so nursing bit the dust very quickly, which was spectacularly short-sighted of me, as it would have been a brilliant career.

Also, aged 17, I got my driver's licence and while friends had cars bought for them, my father pointed me to the nearby bus stop. This made me feel "less than" around my friends and enhanced my "oh woe the fuck is me" self-pity party. I had grown up associating what I had materially with my self-worth. Dad, of course, was perfectly within his rights to limit the use of the car and expect me to pay board. He'd had a life that had been a great deal harder than mine and I'm sure he was just trying to teach me an appreciation for money, but that didn't stop my feelings of resentment or being hard done by. Dad ended up relenting somewhat with the car though and let me borrow it more often than I thought he was going to, which I was enormously grateful for.

I had also learned over the years to associate what I could do and how well I could do it with my self-worth. If dad gave me a task like cleaning and polishing his black work shoes or cleaning his car, I would absolutely go nuts doing the best job possible. I always strived to do my best, even if it was just making my bed. The reward was that dad was pleased with me and this meant a great deal to me when I was growing up. I felt relieved, as I knew dad was unlikely to crap on me for something minor after I'd done something so well. Also, I genuinely got a payback if dad was pleased with me, my self-worth lifted at that moment. I felt better.

So, after Year 12 at MLC, I went to the finishing school in Victoria, Australia, as a border, but I went for the wrong reason. I simply did not know what else to do with myself at the time. I didn't want to go to uni because I didn't know what career to choose, as nothing spoke to me. Unfortunately, I had no vision. I was full of confusion and anxiety about what to do. By going to finishing school, it put off for another year having to try to work all that out for myself. The big wide world frightened me when I was 17 and I didn't know who I was despite dad's parting words of "remember, you are a Thomas." So, my huge ego and low self-esteem took that as meaning I was someone of great importance.

The finishing school experience was mixed. I met some gorgeous girls and learned a lot, but wasn't very happy and put on a lot of weight. This was to be the start of my up and down weight and dieting issues, which continued to plague me for the next few decades.

When I came back to Perth I was 18 and discovered alcohol and cigarettes. I absolutely loved them both. For the first time in my life, I felt ok in my own skin after I had a drink or two and a couple of cigarettes. Better than ok, actually: I felt fantastic, free, and like I could do anything. Alcohol also deadened feelings of being "restless, irritable, and discontent" although, at the time, I wasn't consciously aware of that fact. I just knew I felt better and that's all that mattered. Unknown to me back then, these were three extremely uncomfortable and tormenting traits of the disease of addiction. Alcohol took those feelings away every time and the whole time I was awake, all I could think about was when I could have a drink and a cigarette.

To solve the issue of finding a job, I started working for my father. I didn't like it much. I hated his strictness and I had to spend a tidy sum of my wage on board, which I wasn't thrilled about. I felt entitled to a better deal but didn't get it. However, I still didn't know what else to do with myself. Life completely bewildered me. I had no direction and seemed incapable of finding any purpose for myself. It was like I couldn't think for myself. Plus, I felt like I was just waiting until I met the man I would marry. I had zero vision on how to build a life. I was still very much like a child in many ways.

However, by a turn of good fortune, Ansett Airlines lowered their hostess entry age requirement and applicants no longer had to be a qualified nurse: a First Aid certificate would do and I had one from a course I attended at finishing school. So, aged 19, I immediately applied and became an air hostess. I moved to Melbourne and started a new life, but also started drinking and smoking more in my new found freedom.

Flying was a lot of fun and I started to enjoy life. I usually took one of my scary masks with me on flights to hopefully frighten the crew in the cockpit. On a late-night flight across Australia when the cabin lights were dimmed and passengers quiet, I sat down in the very front row of first-class, which was empty. Not only did I have my creepiest mask with me that night, but I also brought along my horribly ugly rubber claws and feet. I removed my hostie hat and put on the mask, claws, and feet and had just gotten up to walk into the cockpit when a passenger suddenly came out of the front toilet and freaked out when he saw me. I didn't know what to do, so just said hi and walked past him into the cockpit. When I asked the crew if anyone wanted a coffee, the captain was highly amused and insisted on trying it all on himself. This was followed by heaps of photos with him holding the controls with the claws, talking to the First Officer, and trying to drink coffee while wearing the mask. It was a very funny flight.

I also had that same mask with me when I approached a triangle-shaped counter that was in Melbourne's Tullamarine airport departures area when the terminal was first built. I was chatting gaily to the ground hostess behind the counter when I happened to notice two men standing very still at the opposite angle of the triangle. They both were wearing dark sunglasses and were staring at us chatting. No one else was anywhere near us. I recognised them as Paul Hogan and Strop and I remember glancing down at my handbag on the floor and very nearly ducking down to

21

put my mask on, but I just didn't have the courage, so I turned and walked away instead. Sliding door moment.

I did have enough courage though when I had the magician Uri Geller on a flight. He happily followed me around the plane bending spoons for any of the passengers or crew that wanted to see him do it. I also went to the press area after the flight and once I produced spoons that Uri had bent on the flight, the media wanted photos of Uri, me, and spoon. Today I keep that photo on my "famous people that have met me" bookshelf! :)

While flying, I dated a young man that wasn't a pilot. At some point, I transferred from flying out of Melbourne to flying out of Adelaide where he lived and I moved in with the whole family! How generous they were. I was welcomed with open arms. It was a great relationship for some time, but my drinking and my "stinking drinking thinking" were gradually having a negative impact and as I was very homesick, I decided to leave my job, leave him and return to Western Australia.

Not long before I left Adelaide, I had entered a TV Week competition because the second prize was a colour TV, which was new to Australia. However, I won first prize, which was an audition with Crawford Productions in Melbourne, a Pacific cruise for two in the penthouse suite on a Russian ship (from the 13th century), and $250 spending money. When I went for the audition I met Ken James from *Skippy* days. When I was about 13, I had a huge crush on him and wrote him a fan letter. When I told my parents later that I had met him at Crawford's they asked if he had spoken to me. I said, "Yes, he thanked me for my letter."

I had a lot of fun at my audition and met some great people. I passed up a golden opportunity at Crawford's, as I was unwilling to move back to Melbourne, which I needed to do if I was to have a go at a career in TV. However, it would have been a disaster because of my disease of addiction and it also would have completely gone to my head.

Not long after I returned to Perth, aged 22, a close childhood girlfriend Jane and I went on the Pacific cruise together. We certainly had a fun time, but poor Jane had to suffer me sculling Vodka with silver toothed Russians down on K deck for a lot of the trip.

Back in Perth, I then met a really lovely man that I was to marry before I turned 23. The reason for the rush was that I had returned to live at my parents' home after flying and my dear dad was super strict with me. I was not allowed to stay overnight at my fiancé's house. I had to come home. It was completely irrelevant that I would have been way over the limit; that just didn't come into it. Dad had a real thing about me coming home and I couldn't stand it, so we pushed our wedding date way forward.

I really loved this man and at first, I thought our marriage was wonderful. We had some very funny times. And a couple of "royal" times too, which were very special. He was a member of the North Cottesloe Surf Life Saving Club and it just happened to be the surf club that Prince Charles swam at when he visited Perth. The first visit I was involved in was in 1979. Many of us at the surf club were lucky enough to be able to go swimming with the Prince, even my mum and Gillus's mum Dorothy in their flowerpot bathing caps, as Prince Charles came to the beach every morning for over a week, plus on the weekend. It was also the visit where a beautiful model (Jane Priest) came up to him in the surf and kissed him on the cheek, much to his delight.

23

His minders would always call and let the surf club know when he was coming, but late one Sunday afternoon he and his minders turned up unexpectedly. We were all up on the second story of the surf club having a party after a surf carnival when he arrived with his bodyguards and went for a swim. I decided to invite him to the party, so when he walked back up to the clubhouse, I was leaning on the second story balcony railing with a can of beer in one hand and a cigarette in the other and I called out to him to come up for a drink... and he said ok!

After his shower, Prince Charles, Lady Kyall, the Governor's wife, and all the bodyguards came up to the hall above the change rooms. I was at the door to greet them and gave Prince Charles a middy of beer and then proceeded to take him around the room and introduce him to everyone in the hall – from memory, there were at least 100 or more of us. It was completely impromptu: everyone was in shorts and t-shirts, including the Prince. There were no cameras, no mobiles, no press, and no stress. He could relax and have some fun. We had a ball and he stayed for two hours and met everyone there. When he had to leave, he let several of his bodyguards stay on as they were having a great time.

There was a driveway down one side of the surf club, which led to a large paved area in front of the ground level of the club, which is where Prince Charles's car always parked. After his last early morning swim in 1979, and while he showered and changed, I waited outside the clubhouse next to his car to farewell him. When he came out, I said, "I just want to shake your hand goodbye" and he said, "Well, I thought I'd give you a kiss goodbye to thank you" and he leaned forward and kissed me on the cheek. I was absólutely gobsmacked. So were all the Life Savers around and as soon as the Prince left, one of them called out "Let's do a re-enactment, I'll be the Prince, you be Les, etc." True story! And a few days after he left Australia, Lady Kyall came to see me at the beach to thank me and to tell me how much the Prince had enjoyed the party because there was no press and he could completely relax.

Prince Charles came back in 1983 and I went swimming with him again, but this time he was married and the press went nuts. One photo of the Prince and me while we were in the ocean treading water and talking, went around the world. Clearly, there was no other decent news to be reported on at the time, but all the same, my alcoholic brain nearly burst with self-importance.

Over time though, the "restless, irritable, and discontent" traits of my disease ruined my marriage. Not only was I drinking and smoking way too much, but all the character defects of an alcoholic rose up and burst forth like an erupting volcano. I was selfish, self-centered, self-absorbed, self-seeking, inconsiderate, thoughtless, impatient, intolerant, argumentative, rude, arrogant, embarrassing, nasty, jealous, chock-a-block full of my own self-importance, delusional, unkind, and manipulative. I also always felt underlying anger and I had no idea of why I felt like that. Worse, I had a lightning-quick trigger, which would unleash intense and violent verbal abuse on someone if they said or did anything that set it off. I had absolutely no conscious control over this trigger, I immediately lost all contact with whatever part of a rational brain that I had. It was an aggressive fight or flight reaction. I wasn't capable of a sane response. A psychologist I saw for five years in my late 40s and early 50s diagnosed me with PTSD and said she had tried everything, but that my trigger was just too deep, too fast, and too aggressive.

During my marriage, I was also unfaithful and I absolutely hated myself for it. I hated the way I felt, I hated all my character defects,

I absolutely hated who I became when I drank and I hated that I had no control over myself. I couldn't understand why I couldn't stop drinking and couldn't stop behaving like a fucking lunatic. It was so tormenting I could hardly bear being awake sometimes, but only alcohol could take those feelings and thoughts away, so I drank more and more and, in turn, my behaviour got worse. In Alcoholics Anonymous (AA), they call it "self will run riot."

The disease of addiction is a nightmare and I was trapped in self-loathing, as I always thought my behaviour was a moral issue. However, years later in AA, I was to learn that addiction is a disease, that it isn't a moral issue. It is a physical allergy coupled with a mental obsession and it is debilitating. I have a chemical in my brain, which is released when alcohol is put into my system and that triggers uncontrollable obsessive-compulsive behaviour. My body also processes sugar much more slowly than a normal person. That, in turn, speeds up the effects of alcohol in my system. The chemical and sugar overload also completely changes the way I think and feel, so I was in constant fear of myself and of what I might do or say, but I was completely powerless against picking up that first drink because the body's need for the substance was so intense that it had complete control over the mind.

I also learned in AA that I had the emotional maturity of a child: I hadn't grown up. But by doing the AA 12 Step recovery program, I could be returned to sanity… but that was a long way off for me when I was married.

During our six-year marriage, we had two beautiful children who I dragged up on my own after my marriage ended when I was 29. Looking back, I often think that a Power greater than me knew the only way I was going to live through my 30s was if I had children to love and provide for. And He was right. Somewhere deep inside of me was an intense instinct that drove me to go to work to provide a home for my kids. If I hadn't had children, I know in my heart I wouldn't have continued working after my marriage ended: I would have picked up a drink and never put it down again, and would have died of this disease not long after. It had that tight a grip on me.

CHAPTER THREE

Spiralling

Bringing my kids up on my own was extremely difficult for me. Not only financially, but I was constantly tormented by my inability to limit my drinking and smoking. Dad used to say "just stop." This absolutely incensed me and I felt like ramming a red hot iron right up his arse. He had no frigging idea of what I was experiencing and zero tolerance for me not doing what he wanted me to do.

When I was about 30, I moved with my kids into a small unit and walked around the local shopping area asking for work. I managed to get an afternoon in a dress shop, a morning in a fruit shop, a couple of lunchtimes in a restaurant, and an afternoon in a childrenswear shop after persuading the owner that she really should go out for lunch on a Friday and take the rest of the day off. I often did extra days here and there for her too, which was great.

I also had a lot of fun in this job. Late one Friday afternoon, I didn't have time to replace the outfit I'd just sold that the mannequin in the window had been wearing, so I stuck a sign on the mannequin saying "This ensemble is from our invisible collection." Fortunately, my employer was amused when she opened up Saturday morning.

One day, her ex-boyfriend Zelot (not his real name) dropped into the shop while she was doing a hand over to me. He gave me the once over weirdly, which I didn't like, but I thought he must be ok, as she had dated him for a couple of years.

A day or so later he asked me out and, much encouraged by my employer, I agreed. Rather than picking me up, Zelot asked me to come to his home at 7 pm, as it would save time, as he would just have come home from training and I could have a drink while he showered and got dressed.

I thought this unusual, but again thought he must be ok because my employer was gorgeous and she wouldn't go out with a suss man, let alone date him for two years. So, off I went. When I got to his home, he opened the door dressed in tiny shorts and a fitted singlet. The front door opened straight into the living room, so I went in and moved towards the couch thinking I'd just wait there while he got ready. But he suddenly asked if I'd like to have sex. I was so stunned, I just blurted out no and that I needed to use the bathroom. I had to get away from him for a few minutes and gather my thoughts. When I came back into the room, he proceeded to pull down his shorts exposing big Jim and the twins and started to masturbate. I couldn't frigging believe it. He called out that this was all my fault because I wouldn't have sex. WTF! Are you for real? Jaw-dropping moment if ever there was one!

Dumbstruck, I just sat down on the couch. I was quite frightened because of the look of determination on his face. He was going to have his orgasm by hook or by crook and as he was standing between me and the front door, I just stayed still. Fortunately, the TV was on when I came in, so I just watched that until he finished spraying himself all over the carpet. Then I just got up and left.

I didn't mention any of this to my employer. I thought she would go into deep shock or early old age if I did. But a year or so later she said that Zelot had told her what had happened that night. "Oh really," I said, "and what exactly did he say?" She said that Zelot had decided not to date me after all, as he didn't think it would be a good idea because she and I were friendly and I worked in her shop. That infuriated me, so I told her exactly what had happened and she was horrified. He had never behaved like that with her, she said, and it disgusted her to think he was like that.

All the same, I was very promiscuous in those years. I had a full-on affair with a married man. And then another and then another. I was always looking for love in the wrong place and for the wrong reasons. I also thought I had to have sex to experience being held and feeling like someone cared about me. I looked outside of myself for love. I simply did not know that that was the wrong place to look.

At one point during these years, I lost a really good job because of my drinking. I was also broke, so had to sell my car to pay off my credit cards. I spent the next three years riding my pushbike around the area cleaning people's houses and working in gardens to make ends meet. I remember one wintery day when I was riding up a hill it didn't matter how hard I peddled, the rain and wind were pelting so furiously down on me that the bike just didn't seem to be moving forward. I laughed at how ludicrous my situation was, but I still remember thinking at that moment that life just had to get better, didn't it?

Then, out of the blue, my parents bought me a car. I was very surprised and incredibly grateful, but dad spoilt a lot of the joy by giving me a golden coloured chart he'd made with his handwritten list of "Golden Rules" (his title) for what I was and wasn't allowed to do with this car. Some of these rules were so ridiculous, I just wanted to kick his bloody teeth in.

Life still had its amusing times though. When I was working in the fruit shop, a real estate chap used to come in and chat. One day he told me about an experience one of the female reps had. She was a very proper, upper class, slightly snobby, immaculately groomed, and beautifully spoken woman. She had advertised a home open on the weekend and had a call from a man before the opening who asked all sorts of questions about the property and seemed very interested in it. He then asked what time the home was open and if she gave head jobs at that home open. My friend nearly expired telling me how she had told them all this story at their staff meeting in her very cultured voice, very matter of factly with a completely straight face. That story kept me amused for a long time.

When I was about 35, the kids and I had a five day holiday up to Broome with my childhood school friend Jane, her husband and kids, and several of their friends. We would have had more holidays I'm sure if I wasn't an alcoholic and didn't smoke, but at the time, I didn't see it that way at all. We were beyond excited about this trip and had a fantastic time. I've never forgotten it.

My drinking was pretty much way out of control when I decided one Saturday night that I really should have been invited to a private wedding anniversary celebration dinner of an acquaintance of mine: a really lovely girl that I didn't know well, but who was a close friend of a very good friend of mine.

It was her first wedding anniversary and was being held at a restaurant. After several drinks, I thought to myself that I would go. OMG! So off I went and rocked in there and pushed someone half off a seat, so I could sit down on the other half. I can't remember anything of what I said at the table, but I do remember at one point I sat on someone's husband's lap and decided to stay there much to the fury of his wife. At the end of the evening, everyone piled out into the street and I was the last to say goodbye to the anniversary couple and that was when I received a well-placed handbag slammed across my head which sent me straight into the gutter. Unbelievably, I got up and asked what was wrong! OMG! I still cringe. Worse, I followed them home and got out of my car asking again what I'd done wrong. They yelled at me to go away, so eventually, I did.

The next day, in a rare moment of clarity, I was full of remorse and decided the kindest thing I could do would be to stay away from them forever. I only ever saw her again once across a room full of people a year or so later. Our eyes met, but there was no anger in hers, for which I remained forever humbly grateful.

Later in my 30s, I was asked to go on a blind date. When I think of it now, I am reminded of the movie *Blind Date* because it was so similar. I was halfway drunk when I was picked up by my blind date. We were going to the Variety Club Ball and we were to have drinks with celebrities before dinner and would be sitting at a table of celebrities. I vaguely remember some of the early parts of the evening, but from there I proceeded to make an absolute dick of myself until I must have gotten offended by something someone said (no idea what) because I got up saying I was going to the toilet, but I walked out the front door and started staggering down the road. I had no idea where I was, it was pitch black, but after wandering around in the dark for a while, one car came along. It was a cab and it was empty. Talk about a God job. He drove me home. Even worse though, I had been wearing some expensive earrings that a friend had loaned me and I had left one of them on the table. The next day I had to humble myself and apologise to my date and also ring the Variety Club on the off chance they had found the earring. Amazingly, they had, so then I had to go in and get it, cringing the whole time.

When I was 39, I was worried about a friend of mine who I was sure was an alcoholic, as she drank more than me, so I suggested we go to an AA meeting to check out what they do. So, we went, but walked out halfway through and went to a bar. I still remember ordering a brandy and dry, taking a sip, turning to my friend, and saying, "thank God we're not like them." Talk about denial.

After that, I found I hated watching this girl drink, as she drank and got drunk more quickly than me and I didn't like what I saw. What I didn't realise at the time was that she was a mirror for what I didn't like about myself. This was a huge lesson I would learn in years to come. Anything I don't like in someone else is what I don't like in myself. Any comments I take offense to have a hidden truth about myself. This was to become a fantastic way of learning for me, as it was a super quick way to check in with my body. Now and again, I would meet someone and for some completely unknown reason, I would feel the tension in my body and recoil from them. So I would watch what they did and said until I recognised what part of myself they were reminding me of that I didn't like. Then I would work on that defect of character within me and do whatever I could to change and improve. But again, this was well down the track from where I was at 39.

After that AA meeting, I started distancing myself from my friend and I know I hurt her, but I just couldn't stand the mirror.

The crazy thing is that for years I thought I was a really great mother because I loved my children, was going to work every day and I was giving my children a home, food, water, education, clothing, etc. But the truth was that I was a terrible mother. I didn't understand that until I was many years sober and it absolutely cut me to the core. Once I had processed it, I was able to look at myself from my children's viewpoint and I had to acknowledge it was the truth and I felt sick to my stomach, to be honest.

A really weird twist of fate brought me an AA sponsee recently who was having tremendous difficulties forgiving her alcoholic mother. She explained to me why she felt her mother was all sorts of horrible and that her mother thought she'd done a great job as a mother because she'd brought her kids up on her own, went to work, and provided for them. My sponsee just couldn't understand how her mother could think like that and was frustrated that her mother couldn't see the damage she'd done.

I told my sponsee my story about how I had thought the same when I was bringing my kids up and that it will be devastating for her mum when she realises the truth. We have to experience and learn truths for ourselves, someone else can't teach an experience, they can only talk about it and show you what they did. Unfortunately, sometimes it can be very painful.

Compassion and understanding for what others are experiencing and feeling are a couple of the gifts of sobriety and the 12 Step recovery program, but again, that was a very long way down the track for me.

I haven't even started on my weight and dieting issues that were going on at the same time and if I thought my life had been difficult up to that point, it was nothing compared to what was next.

CHAPTER FOUR

The Arsehole
and the Alcoholic

When I was 41, I met a man at a close girlfriend's party. It was a bit of a miracle that I got there actually, as normally I wouldn't have been capable of going anywhere at night. I would already have had too much to drink.

However, my girlfriend Di had asked me to bring a plate, I had said ok and I already organised a sitter for my son, my daughter having gone to live with her dad the week before. This compelled me to make a platter of my "famous to me only" curried egg sandwiches on Saturday morning, which slowed up my drinking somewhat. To this day, I fully believe there were forces at work to get me to this party, as for some inexplicable reason, I slept for the entire afternoon, waking up with only enough time to shower, get ready and go. Even then I was a bit late, but I was sober when I got there.

I still remember standing with Di at the doorway to her dining room. From where we were we could see through the opposite doorway and into the lounge area. At the far side of the lounge area, by the fire, were three people.

A man, Kol (not his real name), facing forward and two other people, one of whom he was chatting to. Di was telling me about him, that he was from another state, a recent widower, a bit younger than us, and visiting friends in Perth. A mutual friend had brought him along that evening. I remember watching his face while he talked and feeling completely disinterested. I wasn't drawn to him at all. Had I taken any notice of my instincts, things would have gone very differently that night. However, I was meant to meet this man and enter a very necessary nightmare – for us both.

Sometime later that evening, purely by chance, I walked into the dining room to get some finger food and he was there alone doing the same. We chatted and he seemed charming and I thought I must have been completely wrong in my first impression of him.

I only remember two other things about that evening. At one point a few of us were lying on our backs on a blanket outside looking up at the stars and he was next to me. He said to me that he thought I was attractive for my age, which made me feel uncomfortable because I sensed he didn't mean it, so I got up and went inside.

Next, I was in one of the bedrooms getting ready to stay the night when I heard Kol talking to Di near the front door, so I went out and asked him to come and talk with me. I've no idea what I wanted to talk about, but we ended up spending the night together in that room.

During the remaining days he had in Perth that week, I saw him again a few times and things developed very quickly between us. This was the start of Kol courting me back and forth across Australia until a few months later he asked me (and my son) to move interstate to live with him with the view to marriage down the track.

What a great idea!

Clearly, we were in love and it was meant to be. I'll just cut down on my drinking a bit, it'll be fine. What could go wrong? I was completely delusional.

In no time at all, we had packed up and moved. A day or so before our flight over though, Kol rang me to say that he expected me to stop smoking when I arrived. A bit late notice! Shock, horror! "Ok!" I said. "Not a problem..." and I was so sure it wouldn't be a problem. After all, I was starting a new life with a wonderful man who said he loved me. And it was too late to not go. I could do this. Why I even thought I had to on his say-so didn't even occur to me.

Within a week of moving, I knew I had made a mistake. And it wouldn't have surprised me if he had felt he had made a mistake too. But I couldn't just turn around and go back to Perth. I had exited a rented home, didn't have a job anymore, and had hardly any money left after the move and paying my son's school fees. I had to give it the best go I could. I was sure I could make it work. And if he had similar feelings, perhaps he thought he'd give it a go too. We just didn't talk about it though.

This was extremely difficult for me, as I was with a man who would be loving towards me one day and then treat me like the scum of the earth the next. I had seen none of this in Perth, nor while he was courting me. He'd always been so lovely, so charming. Once I moved in with him though, everything changed. I bounced from hope to distress and back again depending on what day it was.

However, I didn't stop for a moment to think about things from his point of view. I had not done any work on my addictions or character defects, nor did I think I had a problem, which was hilarious in itself. Also, while he was courting me, I had been on my best behaviour too, so it was hypocritical of me to judge him on that I have to admit.

Plus, I was hiding from him my intense withdrawals from nicotine and to a lesser extent alcohol, as we at least had drinks at night. I was so distressed that all I could think about was how and when I could get some nicotine and more alcohol into me. I was bursting for the relief I knew it would give me. Is it any wonder I started drinking and smoking behind his back, I asked myself?

If Kol and I disagreed though, he would suddenly turn on me with a quizzical look on his face and ask slowly in a very, very condescending tone, "when's your period due?" Always insinuating any problem was caused by me having a period and being over-emotional, no matter how many times a month that might be. Talk about red rag to a bull. Truly, I wanted to rip his frigging head off.

I did have hints of who he was before I moved, but they just didn't register. Perhaps it was the same for him about me. Only one member of his family talked to him. Not his parents, not his brothers, just his sister. One of his brothers had scratched the word C*NT deeply into the back of his Land Rover in huge letters and had also scratched squiggly lines all up the sides of the vehicle as well. How did I overlook all of that? And more importantly, why?

Probably for the same reason he would have overlooked things in me initially. It must have been difficult for him to be lumbered with my strong personality, my addictions, and all my character defects.

I remember him saying to me very soon after I arrived, "you've been here for three weeks and you haven't vacuumed yet and you also haven't even got yourself a job yet." These were things we hadn't even discussed before I left Perth and I was too stunned at the time to remind him he'd told me he had a cleaning lady. There I was, wondering why she hadn't been! He must have dismissed her. It was pretty clear what my roles (plural!) were going to be. I got a part-time job, did everything around the house and garden (cooking, cleaning, shopping, washing, ironing), including doing up the garden with new plantings, cutting the hedges, and washing the car, plus I did all his business's bookwork. I was trying to please him, but who I was at the time had such low self-esteem that I allowed myself to be treated like that. In the not-too-distant future, I'd have to acknowledge that and start addressing it.

Maybe he just didn't know how to deal with the situation if he thought he had made a mistake. Perhaps that brought out the worst in him. I don't know. We just didn't discuss it, so things went on good one day, bad the next.

I used to wake up each day with new hope and motivation that maybe if I did this or that today, it would please him. Unfortunately, it just didn't occur to me that a woman shouldn't have to think like that in a relationship. Nor did it occur to me that perhaps he might be struggling himself having lost his wife only two months before he met me. The awful thing about the latter was that he told the most unbelievable and monumental lie to explain to all his friends and deceased wife's parents about how my son and

I came to be living with him, but I was not to find out about that until not long before I left him and will speak about that a little further along.

There was often some light relief though. His washing line was a rope strung across the back yard between two trees. I complained about this for ages. Eventually, we went to Bunnings and he bought one of those clotheslines where you attach a base to a wall and then the clothesline part could be pulled out and up and would click into place. We got it home and he took it out of its huge box and leaned it up against the fence and that's where it stayed for the next 18 months. About a year after he bought it, we were watching TV one night and an ad came on for a cover you can put over the top of these types of clotheslines to protect clothes from the rain when they are drying. I said to Kol that we really should get one of those for our clothesline and then I completely cracked up, I just couldn't stop laughing, especially when he looked quite put out.

I used to keep lists of all my chores in the kitchen and would cross them off when they were done. Kol always used to check this list when he got home from work and see what I had and hadn't done. One day I wrote in the middle of the list "Admire myself in mirror – one and a half hours" and I had it marked off as done. I nearly expired when he read it. He stood bent over the list for a very long time, but he never said anything about it.

As I mentioned at the start of this book, Kol had a lot of complaints about the food I served up to him. He even complained one day as I was serving dinner, that I had served the same meal three weeks earlier and that I needed to give him more variety. One night though a friend of his came for dinner and commented that he thought we ate like kings. I thanked him very much, but

Kol said nothing. I couldn't see that it didn't matter what I did, nor how hard I tried, this man couldn't possibly have loved me, despite telling me he did.

I would go to great lengths to hide my drinking and smoking – ludicrous lengths. I would always call him to ask when he'd be home from work on the pretext of working out the timing for dinner. He thought I was controlling and I was happy for him to think that. The truth was I just wanted to know how much smoking and drinking time I had. I also took risks with the timing and had many a close shave, but I had my disguises. Just inside the back door was a cupboard and I always kept vegemite and lemon handy to cover my smokers' breath. Also, I had a soft wrap that I put around my hair so that it wouldn't smell of cigarettes and a large al foil ashtray that I could quickly wrap up to hide the ash and butts. Crazy behaviour, but at the time, I couldn't see past my desperate need for relief, not only from the intense cravings for my addictions but also for how I felt in this relationship. I just wanted the pain to go away. It never occurred to me that this was the behaviour of a lunatic and no wonder he was reacting to me the way he was. However, we just went on being the arsehole and the alcoholic.

Once, in the entire three years I lived with him, I decided to give myself a treat and read a women's magazine on the bed when I'd finished all my chores. He came home early and I raced out to the kitchen but made the mistake of leaving the magazine there and not straightening the bed. When he went into the bedroom he called out, "you lazy bitch." There was no "the house looks great and dinner smells wonderful." I simply couldn't see that these were not the actions of a man in love.

His complaints were often extremely petty and were always in a really condescending tone. Like the time he commented in disbelief that there was dust on a thin skirting in the kitchen as he walked in the door from work. It was the first thing he said. I didn't even get a "hello." And you could hardly see the skirting, let alone the bloody dust. Or that he'd noticed I hadn't removed the cobwebs from the high eaves under the veranda roof, for goodness sake! And I still didn't twig that he might have been stressed about our relationship, that I brought out the worst in him.

When I'd drive the Land Rover, he would come out and go around it inspecting it very closely when I got home. He'd then say accusingly "that scratch wasn't there when you went out." The fact that he wasn't even around when I went out wasn't even brought into it. He was just constantly looking for ways to put me down. Or perhaps he just didn't have it in him to tell me the truth of how he was feeling.

I remember one night we were going somewhere in the Land Rover and I was going to be driving for some reason. As we were driving along, we could hear this faint clink clank clink and he wanted to know what I'd done to the car. Of course, it would have to be my fault. However, I decided to stop and asked him to check outside the car, and hooley frigging dooley, he'd left his set of car keys in his door of the car. He went purple. I thanked God that I hadn't done that, I never would have heard the end of it. All I said was, "that could easily have happened to anyone" and drove on. He didn't utter a word about it while I was clenching my whole body trying not to laugh.

One Saturday afternoon, I took my son to see a film. This was the first time I had done this. Big mistake. When Kol came home he was furious, claiming he'd wanted to see that movie and if he was at work on a Saturday, then both of us should be working at home, there was plenty of things needing doing around the house and garden.

The ridiculous thing was that occasionally he would tell me to leave, so I'd start packing. Then he'd come home from work and persuade me to stay, telling me he did love me and I'd think maybe we had a chance. Then when I'd get fed up it would be me saying I was going to leave, then I'd change my mind. I just couldn't seem to get a grip on myself and just go. Perhaps it was the same for him, I don't know.

I absolutely hated it if he wanted to go out for dinner though. He always sat me facing the wall and he would sit opposite so that he could face the room. He would ogle any female that walked by. He didn't just look at women, he would turn his whole head to follow their every move. I'd be talking to him, but he would be staring at the woman passing like she was the only woman he'd seen in 20 years. He was always looking for someone better, younger, sexier. I hated how I felt when this happened. But if I looked sideways at a man or if any of his workmates or friends showed interest in me, he would instantly become possessive, stand up a bit straighter, and look a tad menacing.

I tried to sort out a very large pile of mail that had been on his desk for over two years. He had told me not to touch it when I first started doing his bookwork, but I couldn't stand it any longer and got into it. I couldn't believe what I found. Uncashed Medicare cheques from years ago, all types of bills not paid, mail not answered. It appeared that Kol opened mail, added it to the pile, and then ignored it before I started collecting and sorting it myself. I found this enormously frustrating. But at the time, he found it enormously frustrating that I wasn't being obedient regarding his demand that I don't smoke.

45

To be fair, I had to consider the fact that people who don't have the disease of addiction simply cannot understand the cravings, the insanity, and the compulsive behaviour associated with the disease. So perhaps I could have been more understanding that this was a part of Kol that even he couldn't understand or explain himself. Sometimes people find themselves doing something that they know they shouldn't do, but they do it anyway and are unable to explain why, even to themselves.

At one point, Kol also forbade me from drinking. Laughable really, but I did cut down somewhat. I also managed to quit smoking with the help of patches for quite a while. They took that nasty edge off, which made it possible for me to cope with not smoking. But then something would happen that would stress me right out and I would kid myself that I could just have a few cigarettes to get some relief from the anxiety and then stop again. But, of course, it always turned into another huge battle for me.

One night I said to him that I often thought that God had made the physical attraction between us so strong to keep us together because we both had so much to learn. I also knew, but didn't say, that at some point that connection would break and I knew I needed help to leave.

That came in the form of him seriously threatening my son. Things had been difficult between them for a long time. Ever since my son had shown no interest in going with Kol to his work site and wanted to pursue his passion for film making as his future career. Kol was really annoyed and told him he was an idiot, humiliating him in front of other workmen at the site and telling him he needed to get a real job. Little did he know that my son would wind up with a film on Netflix and the first Stan original documentary series. One of the workmen came up to my son afterward and told him to ignore Kol and go after his dream, which was such a wonderful thing for him to do.

On the day of the serious threat, my son had had an absolute gutfull of Kol being a total prick to him. My son was standing by the glass back door, which opened onto the veranda at one end of the long galley kitchen. I was in the middle of the kitchen between him and Kol. Kol was standing in the doorway to the dining room and had just told my son he was grounded for a week over something ridiculous. For the first time, my son told him to "get fucked" and as Kol launched himself from where he was, my son bolted out the back door. At the same time I immediately put myself between Kol and the door and put up my hands to try to stop Kol. His whole face had gone red he was so incensed and he picked me up like I was a branch off a tree, threw me to the other end of the kitchen, and charged out after my son. I hit the door at the end of the kitchen, fell to the ground, and immediately jumped up and raced out the door. I screamed out at the top of my voice, "run, son, run." I then raced out to the street to see my son was way ahead and there was no way Kol would catch him, as he was already slowing.

Relief, then determination washed over me. That was the last straw. I walked back inside and started packing. My son didn't come back for two days, staying at a friend's house. That was my tipping point because the look on Kol's face had told me he would seriously harm my son if he had caught him. I was never going to let that happen. Nothing was stopping me now and we moved out shortly after on 30 June 1998. I was 44.

CHAPTER FIVE

Divine Guidance

Before we left though, Kol was extremely anxious about all the ways he'd decided that I would take revenge on him. This to me was a ludicrous accusation. He was describing himself, what he would do, and projecting that on to me. Why would I waste my bloody time taking revenge? I just wanted to get away from him. I have always believed in the saying, "vengeance is mine, sayeth The Lord" and told him I didn't need to do anything to him at all, that I completely trusted that a Higher Power would sort him right out.

I felt like an empty shell by the time we moved out, a cardboard replica of myself. I felt like my heart had been ripped out of my chest, chopped up on a chopping board, and cast aside by the back of a hand. I was completely depleted and my soul ached. I knew I had had to leave that man. I wanted to leave that man. I detested that man, but I was experiencing intense physical pain at the separation. It almost overwhelmed me and at the risk of sounding overdramatic, at one point, I just wanted to die.

I knew one thing. I never, ever wanted to experience a relationship like that again, but in a moment of clarity, I knew that "who I was" had attracted him to me. So, I decided I had to change everything necessary about myself so that I never attracted a man like him again.

Firstly, my son and I sat down and wrote down all the blessings from the experience. The main one for him was being able to go to a fantastic school and meeting great new friends. For me, it possibly saved my life because I had stopped smoking for some time during the relationship and I had certainly reduced my drinking. However, both of those addictions, along with my food issues, which I will get to, took off like a rocket as soon as I walked out the door.

A truly hilarious "when I think about it now" thing I did was to make a new list of what I wanted in a man. I'd started going to a church and one of the girls, who was very recently married, said to a few of us girls at a Sunday lunch: "Write down everything you want in a man and make sure you put down absolutely everything. Don't leave anything out. I got exactly what I asked for on my list and I wish I'd asked for more." I was quite struck by that comment but raced home to do my list. It was 11 foolscap pages long. I know, I know – as if! Huge ego, low self-esteem moment. The truly weird thing about it though was that after I had ceremoniously burnt it and sent it up to the universe to get sorted for me, I was overcome by a strange "Oh no, what have I done" feeling and I heard a voice say, "Ok, now we will take the next ten years making you worthy of what you have asked for." My heart sank. Ten years! OMG! Surely not!

During the first year with Kol, I'd found myself occasionally writing letters to "God" asking for help. I was not religious; I just believed there was a God and I knew I needed help. This was to be the start of my relationship with a Power greater than me. My relationship with Kol had been quite traumatising for me, as Kol could be so loving one day and then so vindictive the next, and he never let anyone on the outside see who he really was. I, on the other hand, would scream and yell and argue with him, no matter who was around to see. I'd call him on his shit and get stuck into him without hesitation if he was being unfair to my son or me. And I'd get drunk and generally make a fool of myself, so it was easy for his friends to believe every word he said about me. During the second year with Kol, I had also started to get on my knees to pray sometimes. But in the third year, I was on my knees nearly every day and I was begging for help. Help to get away, as I seemed incapable of leaving myself. I was attached somehow. I can only guess that Kol must have felt he was attached to me too and was possibly just as confounded as to why he couldn't just break free of me.

When we left, going to church over the next few years helped me heal. It took a long time for me to heal, far too long. That helped me realise that there was something fundamentally wrong with my belief system, how I thought, what I was feeling, and why.

I also had to look at my part in that relationship and what it was about me that had attracted Kol to me in the first place. I realised that to some extent we had been necessary for each other because we triggered each other so much and forced each other to look at things about ourselves that we otherwise wouldn't have and we certainly didn't want to.

We were both excessively controlling. He wanted a relationship and he was prepared to work hard to get it, but he didn't want to have to lift a finger to maintain it. I on the other hand insisted on relationship maintenance and we clashed big time over this. When I tried to explain to him that the work a man does to get a woman is nothing compared to the work he needs to do to keep her, his comment was, "you never let a woman know how much she means to you." Ah, whoever said that was a good idea? I told him he would never keep a woman with an attitude like that. A woman likes/loves/needs to be told and shown she is loved, valued, and appreciated. However, I didn't even stop to consider what a man's needs were. It was all about me and what I wanted. No wonder he wasn't interested in doing anything about nurturing and developing the relationship.

After I left, I started to take our relationship apart and look more closely at things like this along with my motives and intentions. This work was hampered though, as I was drinking and smoking again way too much after work each day and on the weekend. I just felt like I couldn't cope without it at the time.

To be honest, I was completely lost for quite some time. I didn't want him back, no way, but I was still attached to him somehow and I was in a lot of physical pain over that attachment, which baffled me. It was so tormenting and I wouldn't wish it on my worst enemy. Also, for the next couple of years, now and again, he would either suddenly turn up at my place or I would find myself contacting him, and I just couldn't understand why I would do that. WTF was wrong with me? I remember saying to him once that I couldn't wait until I was two years down the track from him. I desperately wanted him out of my system and I'm sure he felt the same about me.

Unfortunately, about ten months after we broke up, Kol came to my unit and we had a huge argument, which really upset my son and he moved out. He was only 17. He didn't come back to live with me for several years. I moved to a smaller one-bedroom place, which was a bit of a dump, and lived there for the next three years.

Kol had the grace to feel bad about me having to move again, so he offered to lend me his ute for the move, which I accepted. I can't remember the exact details, but Kol became annoyed with me about something minor (minor in my mind), and he came around to take back the ute before I'd even started moving. I needed the car that day, so I wouldn't give him the keys back, telling him I'd bring it back after my move as previously arranged.

Without me realising it, Kol then removed several of the fuses from the car as he was leaving. I didn't even know cars had fuses. The result of that was that not long after I drove off with a whole lot of my stuff packed up in the tray of the ute, it suddenly stopped in the middle of the street quite some distance from where I had just left. I was beside myself with stress and anxiety and went into a complete panic. I didn't have a mobile back then. I didn't know what was wrong with the car and I didn't know what to do.

Fortunately, the removalists came along and took a look through the ute and saw that some fuses were missing. I just broke down then: burst into tears and bawled my eyes out in the middle of the street in front of these guys trying to move my stuff. I couldn't believe Kol could be so vindictive. Yet, yes, I could believe it. I just wanted to scream my lungs out.

Then, miraculously, a friend from church just happened to come up the street. It was a street she never drove up, she said, and didn't know why she had until she saw me. She also had time to help me, so we took everything out of Kol's ute and went to my new home. The removalists kindly offered to drop Kol's ute keys and the address where the car was back to his letterbox. Unbeknownst to me, they had also taken a few more fuses out, which was dreadful, yet also strangely hilarious.

Unfortunately, though, Kol thought I had done that and went to my new place and removed all of the fuses from the electricity board. OMG! I had no electricity in my new home. And no, I had not told him where I had moved to on either occasion that I moved since leaving him. He had found out about the first place because the post office staff had put my forward mail form in his business post box by mistake and the second time from his sister, who I really liked and had confided in with her assurance she would not tell him. That was a mistake, but I'm sure she had her reasons; she was a really lovely person.

At the same time as all this was going on, I had started seeing a counselor and a psychologist. I had also been reading every self-help and a spiritual book I could get my hands on. I wanted so much to feel better and I knew in my heart that if I stayed close to God and put one foot in front of the other, I would get through the pain I was experiencing.

While I was struggling with that pain, I was also struggling with my addictions and my weight issues. Smoking, in particular, was starting to become a bigger problem, as I was having trouble with my breathing. But of course, I didn't stop: that's how insanely strong addiction is.

My employer extended my hours to full-time when I first moved from Kol's home and my loving Higher Power placed me in a unit that was over the road from where I worked on my second move. Total God job. However, while it was great in that I didn't have to worry about transport or parking costs, I was home just after 4:30 pm each day. To limit my drinking and smoking, I volunteered to look after a lady's garden from the church. I would walk to her home two or three afternoons a week and spend time rearranging her garden, weeding, hand watering, etc. On the other afternoons, I would take myself for a long walk through bushland parks and waterways that were close by. This helped me a lot, but by the time I got home, I couldn't wait to have a drink and cigarette.

Financially, I was not doing brilliantly either. Kol had thought that I would try to strip him of half his assets, but again, he was wrong about me. I wasn't interested in his flipping assets, I just wanted to get away from him. Freedom was way more valuable to me. However, I was in a job that paid a very low wage, I didn't have a car for five years after I left him, and I was on the bones of my backside most of the time. But, I was free and that was worth more. I was to learn in time that it's all about how you feel on the inside even though I didn't recognise my relief as that back then.

The unit I rented – which was the front half of a very old weatherboard house – had no central heating and loads of small holes in the walls. In winter, it was like an ice bucket. I did have a small heater, which I used to sit right in front of at night. I lived there slowly recovering for the next three years.

I knew this was a ridiculous length of time to be recovering from a tormenting relationship, but I had a lot of other issues that needed to be addressed and worked on. This prompted me to revisit the most humiliating thing that had happened while I was with Kol.

Kol told the most monumentally false story, a blatant lie, to his deceased wife's parents and all his friends about how my son and I came to be living with him. As I mentioned at the start of chapter four, we "fell in love" and he asked me to come and live with him and we'd look at marriage down the track. However, not long before our relationship ended, I found out that what he had told these people was a completely different story.

He told them that we had met in Perth and that we had visited each other interstate several times. Then, out of the blue, without speaking to him about it, I'd moved myself and my son across the country and into a flat around the corner from where he lived. Then a few weeks later, while he was at work and without his knowledge or permission, I had moved myself and my son into his home and that there was nothing he could do about it. Word for word, I kid you not! OMG! I absolutely couldn't believe it. I was incensed. What an absolute arsehole. No wonder those people had been so weird and cold with me. Now I understood why, but there was nothing I could do about it. I didn't have any of their phone numbers and Kol always put on such a show for them all of what a great bloke he was, they would never have believed me even if I could contact them to tell them the truth. So, as infuriated as I was, I had to just cop it and let it go.

I have always believed that the truth always comes out sooner or later in life. We humans can say whatever we like, but we always end up showing other people who we are by our actions.

One of Kol's friends, Julie (not her real name) had also left an angry phone message for him saying, "that individual you are with is soooo sick." I was stunned. I hardly knew this girl. Kol argued that she was upset about me being with him because she had missed out on her chance with him, which I sensed was a load of rubbish. It was because of what he had said about me to her.

And I couldn't get what she had said about me out of my head. My ego was screaming "how dare she." The fact that she had been spot on about me completely escaped me at the time. She was right. I *was* sick. Mentally, emotionally, physically, spiritually, and financially.

There was so much I had to work on and I didn't even realise it.

At some point, I decided to go to Bunnings and get some Christmas lights to put up on a big tree out the front of my unit. I also wanted some tomato, cucumber, and capsicum seedlings to grow in the front garden, as it was a very sunny spot. Bunnings was a fair hike, but I enjoyed the walk. I also bought a large spade, which I thought I could carry on my shoulders with bags of seedlings and Christmas lights balanced at either end. It sounded like a good plan to me, but I ended up having a huge laugh at myself, as I had to stop so often on the way home, as the load was killing my shoulders. I did get home though and I thoroughly enjoyed planting my seedlings and putting up the Christmas lights. I climbed to the top of the 30-foot tree holding the middle of the long string of coloured lights and attached that bit to the very top of the tree. Then, using a neighbour's borrowed ladder on either side, I managed to shape the lights on both sides of the tree to come down in layers, so it really did look like a well-shaped Christmas tree from the road. I was so frigging proud of myself.

Planting my seedlings, watching them grow, being able to enjoy that tree with the sunlight glistening through it in daylight and those beautiful lights at night gave me enormous pleasure every day and every night and made me feel something on the inside of myself again.

I knew my healing had begun.

CHAPTER SIX

Unlocking a Door

The end of my relationship with Kol marked a major turning point in my life. I had to be in excruciating mental, emotional, and physical pain to trigger change within me on a much deeper level. I simply wasn't one of those people who immediately recognised something that was not good for their wellbeing and did something about it straight away. I had been running around unconsciously leaving a trail of destruction behind me since early adulthood and I had carelessly and thoughtlessly plowed through people, places, and things along the way.

From the age of 45 onwards though, I started to climb out of the quicksand-like pit of despair. My progress was certainly slow, hampered by my disease and overload of character defects, but some amazing things happened and some truly miraculous things happened as I moved slowly forward, all of which I will talk about as my story progresses.

My healing took a long time because I had so much to deal with and overcome. However, looking back, I needed to go through everything that I did in order to receive the most incredible recovery and healing. Sometimes I would fall back down, but I was driven to pick myself up and keep going. I had to and I had to address my addictions, overcome past traumas, and learn a new way of living and a new way of thinking and feeling. I also needed to find a way to remove or change ingrained beliefs that were either just plain wrong or just didn't work for me. If I had been a lot smarter and a lot more self-aware, my healing would have been a great deal faster, I am sure.

I have hardly mentioned my beautiful daughter, who visited us from Perth when we lived with Kol and who came interstate to live after we left him. I've mentioned my son a fair bit in a previous couple of chapters, but overall and as much as possible, I will only mention my gorgeous kids when it's important or relevant.

In 1999 and 2000, I was gradually having more serious difficulties with my breathing. It became so bad that I couldn't even lie down in bed at night. I had to lie upright with a lot of pillows and cushions behind me. Even though I could hardly breathe, my insane cravings for nicotine had me coming back for more. I just couldn't understand why it was that I logically knew I needed to stop smoking, yet couldn't. It made no sense at all that my body completely ruled my mind.

I made myself limit my smoking by wearing a Nicorette patch at work during the day but would rip it off and light up as soon as I got home. Then I would just plow straight into more. I tried to further limit myself by only smoking outside and this helped somewhat. However, it didn't stop me. Nor did lashing rain, hail, or thunderstorms outside. I'd just put up an umbrella.

Speaking of an umbrella reminds me of the time I invited a girlfriend from church over for dinner. By the time she had arrived, I had already had quite a bit to drink. As a huge treat, I had bought a whole fillet of steak to roast with vegetables in the oven. However, my friend Julie arrived just as the fuse for the oven blew. I replaced the wire in the fuse, but for some unknown reason, the oven wouldn't come back on. So I told Julie to sit down and watch TV while I got the BBQ going out the back and that I would just cook it all on that. Unfortunately, it was pouring down with rain outside, teeming down in fact, and there was no outside light, which made it difficult. So, there I was out there in complete darkness except for a low battery torch, holding an umbrella over the BBQ trying to cook, smoke, and drink all at the same time.

At some point I must have decided it was cooked and put everything on a plate, covered it in alfoil and came inside. I popped into the lounge to tell Julie it wouldn't be long now and went back to the kitchen.

After quite some time of trying to find where I had actually put the plate full of food, I went back and stood in the doorway of the lounge, apparently with a bewildered look on my face. Julie asked "Where's dinner?" and I said, "I can't find it."

"What?" She couldn't believe it and didn't know whether to laugh or cry, but came out into the kitchen to help me search. Dinner had completely vanished. I knew I had brought it in, but do you think we could find it? On the point of thinking I'd have to make some sandwiches, Julie opened the microwave and low and behold, there was dinner. I have no idea what possessed me to put it in there, but we sure laughed about it for a very long time.

As I continued on in the first half of 2000, my attempts to stop smoking were hampered by low self-esteem, lingering painful withdrawal symptoms from the codependent relationship I had been in, a lack of any real purpose or direction in my life, and general bewilderment about myself and my situation. Also, somewhere deep inside of me, I recognised that I just didn't feel good about myself: I had no self-love and I felt uncomfortable in my own skin. Clearly a low point in my upward journey, but it's important to acknowledge how my mental state and lack of self-awareness hindered my progress and stifled my motivation to make the monumental effort each day to try to quit. Smoking was a reward for getting through the day to me. As ridiculous as that sounds, it was very true for me back then, so it was a daily battle and, more often than not, I found myself clinging to my alcohol, nicotine, and comfort food crutches like there was no tomorrow.

However, I just kept working at it. I read many self-help books, did several personal development courses, and was seeing a counselor regularly. It was a huge battle every day for me. I did everything I could to stop smoking under my own steam, but it was impossible and I felt like I was going insane. Not even the difficulty breathing at night could stop me. I used to say out loud "what the fuck is wrong with me" over and over again. I had no idea I had a disease at the time. I just thought I must be useless.

Every morning I would be on my knees at the side of my bed begging for help to quit. Often, I would bawl my eyes out in pure frustration. I persisted though. I was at the point where I thought I was going to tear the skin off my arms in absolute insane frustration when suddenly one day, while I was sitting on the ground in my little front garden wondering if I would ever be able to stop for good, a very unusual sensation came over me. Everything went still and quiet for a moment and I became aware of a presence. Suddenly, I knew I would never smoke again. The desire and compulsion for nicotine had been removed by something with immense power. I could feel it leaving me and it was like it was lifted up and carried away by a light breeze, brushing through the branches and leaves of my beautiful Christmas tree and on into infinity. I was awestruck. It was a truly magical and miraculous moment.

I became overwhelmed with immense gratitude and relief. I couldn't believe it and I wept. I simply did not want a cigarette at all and I never touched one again. It was June 2000 and I was 46.

Now I had proof a miracle was possible. Even though all of life is a miracle, this was something else. I had physically and consciously experienced something impossible for me to do as a human.

On 18 September 2000, another amazing thing happened. It was the night I saw Kol for the last time. My dear friend Rainey from work invited me to the Johnny Farnham Man of The Hour concert at the Rod Laver Arena in Melbourne. I remember having a super weird feeling on the way there in the car with Rainey and I told her about it. Rainey could see I was on edge and we sat and talked about it before going into the arena. I knew something was going to happen and I felt extremely uneasy.

Before going into our seats, we sat out in the foyer area and had a few drinks. While Rainey was getting our last drinks, I happened to look up and through the huge glass walls into the distance. There was a covered walkway a long way away that lead from a car park to the arena where I was. As I looked at the walkway, I saw lots of people, but one walking stride caught my attention, and even though I couldn't see the people clearly, I recognised it. It was Kol. However, there were hundreds of people around and I doubted we would bump into each other, so thought my preconceived uneasiness had been unfounded.

A little while later the bell went for us to go in, so Rainey and I stood up and started walking across a short area towards the door we were to enter. Suddenly, from behind a support pylon on the left two people stepped out and came forward towards us. They were walking against the flow of people and looking directly at me, so it appeared they had been waiting for us to get up to go in, so that they would cross our path. It was Kol and a young woman. I looked straight into Kol's eyes. I suspected he wanted me to see him with another woman either to let me know he had well and truly moved on or he might have thought I would be jealous. I wasn't. Something – I always thought an Angel – kept me calm and kept a relaxed expression on my face. It was quite amazing actually. I didn't say anything to Kol at all, but I noticed his expression change as we walked past. He now looked uncomfortable. I did look back over my shoulder after a few moments and I saw the girl jumping up and down excitedly chatting to him, but he had a tenseness to his body and wasn't responding and I sensed he might have regretted what they had just done.

Once inside, Rainey and I went to our seats: about row 19 from the front on the flat floor area. Then a friend of Rainey's came to our seats and told us to go and see the sound guy, who was situated at the back of the flat area but on the other side to where we were. He had some after-party passes for us, organised by Rainey's muso brother and hubby so that we could go backstage after the concert and attend the party. So, as people were walking into their seats all around the arena, we walked to the back and across to where the sound guy was checking all his equipment. While Rainey was chatting to him, I casually glanced around the arena and immediately spotted Kol and his friend. They were sitting in the tiered area, directly behind and higher up from where our seats were. I was glad I knew where they were and I was glad he would have to look at my back all night. Rainey and I then walked back to our seats.

When Johnny Farnham sang "I Burn For You," I felt like there was a hot beam focused on my back. I could physically feel that connection between us intensely pulling at me, but I just sat there looking straight ahead. I knew then I would never see him again. I knew he wouldn't contact me after that night and I knew I would never contact him again either. I was greatly relieved even though I still felt the pain. I could move forward now. To me, how that night played out was absolutely miraculous.

In January 2002, I got a great new job in the city, which was another God job, as it was through a friend and was handed to me on a platter: Administration Manager and PA to the Managing Director. I was so fortunate and it paid about double what I had previously been earning, so things were looking up. It also meant I could move to a nicer and bigger unit. I was even able to buy a secondhand car in 2003, plus my son also moved home for about a year, which was wonderful. Things went well in my new job, but there was a fabulous bar and light lunch restaurant over the road and it wasn't too long before I was racing over there every lunchtime. Every morning I would be determined not to go there, but by halfway through the morning, I couldn't wait to get there. I was in a good intention-failure-guilt cycle with my drinking.

I was also on my knees every morning and night begging for help to control my drinking. I didn't really want to stop, I just wanted to feel better and be able to control the number of drinks I had. I knew I was in a lot of trouble though because I had zero control over how much I drank and, at the same time, it was inconceivable to me to live without it. I was on the edge and risked sliding back into that pit of despair.

A bit of light relief came in the form of a three-night weekend trip to Hamilton Island to attend a John Gray "Men are From Mars, Women are From Venus" workshop. It was a terrific workshop with only 45 people attending, so we each had one on one time with John, which was fantastic. A really interesting thing happened though. John asked a lady in the group a question and she proceeded to give a whiney account of how 20 years ago on her honeymoon in South Africa, she had been bitten by something and how she had ended up in a hospital and how it had affected her every day since. I noticed her husband's expression when she started up on this story and it was an "oh no, not again" look of total exasperation. When the girl finished, John Gray said, "I see that thing is still biting you 20 years later."

I didn't realise for many years that she had been whining the way I had whined for years about my life to anyone who would listen. I had lived in a victim mentality for most of my life and realising that was a huge shock.

I had a wonderful time though and because the workshop went all day and late into each night, I hardly drank and felt fantastic. However, as soon as I was home, I was straight back into it. So, in 2002, I went to my first AA meeting in Victoria, some ten years after my very first AA meeting in Western Australia. After being there about ten minutes though, I thought, "no, this isn't for me" and didn't go to another meeting until the next year. Even then, I think I only did a couple of meetings in 2003.

Also in 2003, my dear friend Di from Perth came over to Melbourne to take me, my son, and another friend of ours, Jude, to a Beach

Boys concert. She knew one of the band members and had arranged for us to arrive early, go backstage to meet the band, and spend some time with them before the show. Over 20 years earlier when I had been married, my ex-husband and I had gone to a Beach Boys concert. I had lined up very pregnant for hours to get seats a few rows from the front. At one point in the concert, the drummer had thrown his sticks into the crowd and I had caught one of them. Unfortunately, though, it had been stolen from our home back then.

Di had already organised two more drums sticks from the band for me and they all signed the sticks while we were backstage. My son sent one stick to his dad and I kept the other one. We had a fantastic time that night, got lots of great photos and I felt so privileged to meet them. The concert was brilliant; I have always loved their music.

My drinking continued to get worse though and 2004 was a really bad year. Firstly, the company I worked for in the city was sold and the entire staff was made redundant in January of that year. I spent the next couple of months trying to get another job, but also drinking more because I was at home a lot and terribly distressed about my unemployment and financial situation. Long story short, I was mentally, emotionally, physically, spiritually, and financially bankrupt at that point. Plus, I had put on 23 kilos from comfort eating, which just added to my depressed state.

Applying for and being rejected from positions vacant can be extremely deflating and trample your self-esteem. I was also doing my best to present myself as bright, capable, and happy and this was a huge strain, especially when I was continually unsuccessful at getting a new job. Also, while I had loads of experience and was very capable, I had no formal qualifications. Finally, in March

2004, through my good friend Rainey, I got an introduction to a media sales position and got the job. It was not a great position in that I didn't spring out of bed in the morning bursting to get to work, but I was enormously grateful and I strived to do my best in the job.

Christmas 2004 was an absolute disaster. I went to Perth to see my parents, lifelong school friends, and family. On two occasions though, I got blind drunk to the point of operating in blackout. To this day, I have absolutely no recollection of what happened on either occasion, but I really upset my dear friend Di, who I was staying with and another lifelong buddy Jill at a dinner out, and also my younger brother when I went to his home. None of them spoke to me again for a very long time.

So, when I came back to Melbourne in January 2005, I knew I had to do something. Clenching my teeth hard and nearly going out of my frigging mind with the insane cravings, I forced myself to not drink Monday to Friday and started going to AA every Thursday night at a local meeting. I hated AA initially, but I went. If I was asked to share at the meeting, I always said the same thing: "I grit my teeth Monday to Friday and absolutely claw my way through the week nearly going insane not drinking, but I race straight to a bottle shop after work on Friday and stock up for the whole weekend. I just can't understand how any of you people can go through a weekend without a drink. I certainly can't."

To me, it was unfathomable, inconceivable, and impossible and I knew at that point that this was as good as it was going to get for me under my own power.

I needed another miracle.

CHAPTER SEVEN

Empowering Gift

In July 2005, I received a truly wonderful gift and a magical break from my tumultuous life. My lifelong friend Jane, whom I have known since I was four years old and who had come with me on the Pacific Cruise I won in my early 20s, took me to Bali for five days of luxury. We stayed at a gorgeous luxurious spa hotel. It had several pools and also the largest spa in the southern hemisphere. It was enormous, about a quarter acre and it took two hours to work our way around all the different sets of jets for all parts of the body. I have to say I went cross-eyed at a few of those jets much to the amusement of the Chinese girls behind me. They couldn't stop giggling at my facial expressions of jet delight.

Five days of healthy living, swimming, relaxing by the pool with a good book, having a massage or spa, and eating the most delicious food was like being in heaven for me. I loved every minute. It was the most incredible hotel, situated high on a cliff overlooking the ocean. I was so grateful for that holiday: it was so generous of my friend and when I think of it today in 2020, it was like an oasis of light in my dark life back then showing me how much better things could get if I got well.

In October 2005, my son, who also has the disease of addiction, came back home to live again. Now I found I was trying to hide the extent of my drinking from him and it wasn't easy. I knew I wasn't fooling him, but it didn't stop me from trying. I had a few "tells." One of which was that one of my pupils expanded to double its size when I had a drink. You'd think that would cause me concern, but no, I didn't even speak to my doctor about it.

I continued going to AA in the second half of 2005, but not as much. I just wasn't getting the AA message. I was looking at the differences between myself and others at meetings, instead of the similarities. I also hadn't tried to get myself a sponsor, nor was I prepared to do the AA 12 Step recovery program at that time.

I thought that because I had already done so many self-help courses, I just wasn't up for another one. Plus, I was seeing a counselor and we were working through my issues and I felt that was all I could cope with. I remember reading the AA 12 Steps of Recovery on a large banner on the wall at my Thursday night meeting and thinking to myself that that was enough – which was ludicrous, of course, I just didn't know it at the time. Upon reflection, had I known the extent of what was involved in actually doing the 12 Steps, especially doing a moral inventory and making amends to people I had harmed in my life, I probably would have walked out the door, so perhaps it was for the best that I didn't know at the time. Lessons come when we are ready for them, as do our teachers, and I needed to become teachable first where AA was concerned.

To be honest, I was still in hell. I had been on my knees for years begging for help to stop my drinking and nothing was happening. I could hardly stand being awake; I was so tormented. The fact that the answer was glaring me in the face completely escaped me at the time.

Then my daughter moved home in early January 2006. She also had the disease of addiction, but she was two years clean and sober and when she walked up the front steps to move in, I remember being struck by how absolutely fantastic she looked. So healthy, so vibrant, so alive and so happy within herself. I wanted that too, but up until then, I had been unwilling to do the work required.

My prayers changed immediately though to include, "I'm willing to be changed and I'm willing to do your Will for me and anything I've been unwilling to do, I'm willing to be made willing." I didn't think I could get more willing than that!

My daughter didn't tell my son and me to get sober, nor how to get sober. She showed us the way by her actions. I watched her. She had daily conscious contact with her Higher Power. She talked regularly to her sponsor and encouraged her sponsees on the phone, she went to regular AA and NA meetings and she took up service positions at meetings. She also did the 12 Step recovery program in both fellowships. I went to a few meetings with her and listened to her speak when she got up to share her experience, strength, and hope. Although I balked at the work in front of me, I was so terrified of myself by then, I knew I was becoming willing to do almost anything to get sober and that gave me hope.

It's really like being two people having this disease. One believed she has a good heart and desperately wanted to get sober, the other was a total nightmare.

71

All these years, every morning was the same. I would wake up feeling like death warmed up, unbelievably hungover, swearing I would never drink again, crawl out of bed, and down onto my knees at the end of the bed. Crying and begging God to do something about me because I just wasn't capable of controlling my drinking myself and I was certainly not capable of stopping on my own.

On the morning of 21 March 2006, I said something slightly different in my prayers. I had been hanging on to my job, the unit I was renting, and the car I was paying off, but this morning I felt myself let it all go. I surrendered everything. I could feel it in my body. And I said to God that he could have all these things: I'd give them up, I'd go and live in an AA Oxford house with other alcoholics, I'd do nothing else but go to meetings, get a sponsor, do the steps, do service work, I'd do anything, absolutely anything to have this removed from me. I was completely and utterly done.

Then I felt that silence and quietness again and I heard a voice say, "I've searched your heart and see you are speaking your truth. You can keep your car, your unit, and your job and I will take your disease." Then I felt a hand go into my chest and pull something out. I suddenly felt different and began tapping my chest with my hands saying out loud, "it's gone, it's gone, it's not there" and I burst into tears of relief. I was completely overcome with emotion that someone would help me, someone as unworthy as me. That God would help a wretch like me. His Grace is truly amazing. The desire for alcohol had been removed and I have not touched alcohol since. I was 52.

Once again, I was in awe of being given a truly miraculous gift. Another miracle. Wow! Thank you, God, with all of my heart. I could hardly believe it had actually happened and all I wanted to do then was honour this gift by doing everything I had to do to keep it. I immediately got myself a sponsor and started doing the steps. I also joined another AA group and volunteered to be their treasurer. I went to extra meetings and did everything my sponsor suggested to me, including ringing her every morning at exactly 9 am to check in with her.

One thing I couldn't wait to happen though was for my kids to stop searching my face for my "tells" to see if I'd had a drink. I hated seeing that look on their faces. It was so, so wonderful when that stopped. It meant they trusted that I really was sober and would stay sober.

When thinking about that, I recall the first night of my sobriety. I had gone to bed, but I was still awake. My daughter was still up and then my son came home. I heard my daughter telling him that I hadn't had a drink. My son immediately came down to my room and even though it was fairly dark, I could see he was checking the floor just under my bed where my head rests. He thought I was asleep and was looking for the glass of wine that had been there every night in the past. There wasn't a glass of wine there that night and I am fairly sure I heard him weeping as he left the room. And I felt absolutely sick to my stomach that addiction is far stronger than a mother's love for her kids.

I remember recalling my son as a little boy. What an absolute darling he was, as was his beautiful sister. One particular occasion though came to mind that night. My son had asked me for a Scalextric set (race car set of tracks and cars). We had been standing facing each other in the small lounge room where we lived back then. I told him that there wasn't enough room in that lounge room to swing a cat by its tail, let alone set up a Scalextric set. He looked very thoughtful for a while, then suddenly looked up at me all excited and said, "well, don't let the cat in." I completely cracked up and him saying that with such a delighted "I've got the answer" look on his face kept me going for years. I've never forgotten it.

That night though, realising in a one-day sober state of how deeply I had hurt my children through my drinking and outlandish behavior over the years was extremely gut-wrenching and tormenting in its own way. I didn't even know the full extent of how deeply I had harmed them for many, many years, and not even learning that alcoholism was a disease and not a moral issue stopped the shame and guilt. I said to a friend once that I felt like I had paid over and over and over again for all the mistakes I made and hurts I caused. I knew I was punishing myself, but at that time, I had not learned how not to yet.

Miraculously, four months after me, my son received a miracle too and became clean and sober in one weekend. For the next 12 months, both of my kids lived with me and this really helped to strengthen my sobriety and hopefully theirs too.

With sobriety came motivation and hope for my life. One thing I was determined to do was to be, from that moment on, the best mother, daughter, sister, friend, and work colleague that I could be. I certainly fell down many times, but I always got back up again and kept doing my best. I had to.

I continued with the 12 Step recovery program, which I found extremely confronting. It forced me to look much more deeply at myself and also to look at myself as others saw me. Making amends to my children, family, friends, and others who I had harmed in my life was an extremely humbling experience. Although making these amends to people close to me was all about what I had done to them, since then, if the need to make amends arose, it was sometimes difficult in that I could only talk about "my part" in whatever had taken place. In AA, there is none of the, "well I did or said this to you because of what you did or said to me." That's a big no no! An amends can only be about my words, my actions, my wrongs, my part. I only look after my side of the street and never mention the other person's part. It becomes difficult when the other person either can't see their part or won't admit their part. Difficult because sometimes I have, or at least my ego has had, expectations of them doing so. This was wrong of me, as it takes the humility and truth out of the amends and puts my expectations in. So in those instances, I had to do extra work on myself, truly humble myself, make my amends honestly and from the heart, and let it go. I had to and as time passed I learned a really beautiful way of doing this, which I will talk about further along in my journey.

After getting sober and doing the steps, I thought it was about time I got myself a boyfriend, so I joined a couple of online dating sites. OMG! What an experience that was.

At the time, all the men my age that I was drawn to were only looking for someone ten to 20 years younger and the only men interested in me were ten to 20 years older than me and were mainly looking for someone to look after them and their home. I almost got the feeling my profile photo should have me holding a mop and bucket with the vacuum cleaner and perhaps the odd duster in the background.

I only ever arranged to meet a man for a half hour coffee. I knew I would know straight away whether or not there was any chemistry between us or not and I didn't want to spend a long time with someone I knew I wasn't going to see again, so the half hour seemed about right to me.

One man I met picked up my hand and examined it, and said he was glad I had the hands of a working woman not afraid to look after the home. He went on to say he didn't want to get involved with a woman who had her hands pampered.

Another chap looked at least 15 to 20 years older than his profile photo and when I asked him about that he said, "if I had put up a true photo, you wouldn't have met with me." I told him that was true, but that as he had to lie to get me there, I had no respect for him and wouldn't meet him again anyway. He thought about that for a moment before saying, "oh, I hadn't thought about that."

I also met one man around my age, but he had a ten-year-old child from a second marriage to a much younger woman and now he wanted a woman to look after the child. No younger women would, so he thought he'd go for an older woman.

Then I met a man who seemed ok at first, but after a while, I noticed he was staring at my lips. How frigging embarrassing. I hate my lips; they are so thin and only look ok if I am smiling. Plus I refuse to fill them up with anything, as I hate the fish pout look. After a while, I asked him why he was staring at me and he said, "I was just wondering what it would be like to kiss you." OMG! I nearly threw up into my handbag. Needless to say, that half hour was a short one.

But it was the man who told me all the good and bad things about the last person he dated from the website that took the cake. For some reason, he seemed to think I needed to know that this woman had never farted in his presence and I could see by the look on his face and his tone of voice that he was still fascinated by this fact. For me, it was a "mouth open catching flies" moment. He also said that she had always made sure she painted her fingernails and toenails, which he said was very important to him. OMG! Really!

By this time, I was starting to get an inkling that I was not attracting the right sort of man, so maybe I needed to do some more work on myself before going any further. So, I went offline.

It was a long time before I understood why I was attracting those sorts of men. It was my attitude and expectations that were the cause. I wanted something from a man and these men were looking for women that would provide what they wanted too. It was completely the wrong way to go about it, but I just didn't know that at the time.

It would be many years before I fully understood that a man and a woman (or man/man, woman/woman) should be complete within themselves, have a deep sense of who they are, have self-love and be solely responsible for their own happiness. Also, unless in extraordinary circumstances, be responsible for their own financial wellbeing and not put unrealistic expectations onto each other. Basically, be a bonus in another person's life, rather than a needy lead weight, which is exactly what I would have been at the time.

I had gone onto those dating websites for the wrong reasons. I was still of the mindset that I had grown up with: that a man provides for the woman financially. And the men I attracted wanted a chief cook and bottle washer, a housekeeper and/or a childminder – and I wondered why I was put off.

Around this time I also started going to a swimming pool for some exercise. Each time I went, there was a lovely old man there with white hair and a long white beard wearing great big board shorts to his knees as bathers. I thought he was the epitome of Father

Christmas and that he would have looked good under my fairy light Christmas tree out in the front garden at my previous address. When he started chatting to me, I didn't think much of it. I thought he was just being friendly. One day though, he swapped his big baggy board shorts for skin-tight red budgie smugglers and I remember being taken aback. I was even more shocked when I was resting in the water at the end of the pool after a big swim and he came to stand right over the top of me at the very edge and started chatting. When I looked up to answer, I copped a whopping eyeful and my eyes started flickering involuntarily in shock. My jaw dropped at the same time taking in water and as I looked away my eyes rolled to the back of my head and I started choking and coughing from the water intake. I couldn't frigging believe he would stand there like that. Then he had the gall to ask me out on a date. I was stunned. WTF? He must have been 80 or 90. I swam away like a rocket, flew out of the pool at the other end in a single bound, and never went back again. After that, I was a tad put off by the idea of dating for quite some time.

At some point, I made my amends to my two dear friends Di and Jill and my younger brother in Perth. I was so fortunate to have them all back in my life. A really difficult amends to make though was to my ex-husband from my 20s. By this time, he had met and married a really lovely lady and they were very happy and living overseas. I have to say I was genuinely so very pleased that he had found someone so worthy of him. I had felt like the worst woman on planet Earth for years because of who I was when I was married to him. Sometimes back then I wondered if guilt and shame could ever be healed. I was to come to learn that it certainly could, but that was still a long way off for me.

Early 2008, I started a new job with another media organisation and while I still had personal issues to deal with over the years to come, it was the start of me going deeper within and learning more about myself, self-care, self-love, life, spiritual growth, health, fitness, food and weight issues and, most importantly, about forgiveness and what it really means.

However, unbeknownst to me at that time, I also had other hidden addictions to do with food to overcome. Luckily though, I had some spectacular adventures and some truly amazing and magical happenings along the way that kept my spirits uplifted.

These Heaven-sent blessings left me in no doubt whatsoever that there is life after our earthly death and that Angels are real.

CHAPTER EIGHT

The Magic in the Mirror

A mirror is an amazing thing. It reflects our beauty if we smile and it reflects our pain if we are hurt.

A human mirror though is something else entirely and can be both wonderful and frightening.

When I can set my ego aside, a human mirror is a most valuable asset for it tells me about myself.

As part of my recovery from the disease of addiction, I have had to look at myself and my behaviours far more deeply on an ongoing basis. I have also had to be honest with myself about my character defects and all the damage I have done in the past.

When I apply acceptance and willingness to this, I can make great progress. And I make remarkable progress when I am willing to see the magic in the human mirror. As I mentioned much earlier, if I don't like something someone has said or done, rather than being annoyed, I need to recognise myself in that person's words or actions. I will always find myself in there if I look honestly.

Oddly enough, when I see myself and recall my actions when I behaved in the same or similar way as my offender, compassion rises in me. I have a measure of understanding then as to why the person acted the way they did. This in turn makes forgiveness a lot easier.

It has also been an enormous help to me because I genuinely want to be a better person. So, if I feel an intake of breath or a stronger reaction to what someone has said or done, I observe that person until I recognise myself.

However, in early sobriety, it didn't work too well. Actually, it hardly worked at all. As I mentioned a lot earlier on, I have a trigger that is lightning fast and I have never had any control over it. When triggered, I would immediately be disconnected from my rational brain and become ten times worse than the monster from the deep.

I found it impossible to calmly observe someone who had just upset me in those instances. Mostly, I would aggressively fly off the handle, especially in a work situation when someone else's actions impacted my income. This alienated me from people and it made me very sad because I hated it too. But I especially hated other people's responses to it. I felt like a freak. I remember one young chap at work turning to me and saying "just count to ten," which sent me into a tailspin as I pulverised him into the carpet.

But as the years rolled on, my trigger has been lessening and healing. However, it is always in the back of my mind and still makes me very nervous about letting new people in.

A beautiful gift about the mirror though is that there are people that I know or new people I have come across from time to time that I am instantly drawn to in a very big way or instantly feel completely at home with and feel great joy in their presence. These people are showing me the love within me. It has always given me great hope when I recognise something I like or enjoy about myself in someone else.

However, something happened to me whenever I went to Perth to see family and friends. I immediately, and completely involuntarily, became and behaved as a child again, especially around my father.

Christmas 2008 I went to Perth to attend a dear friend's wedding. It was a beautiful wedding on the foreshore of the Swan River late one summer afternoon, followed by a wonderful reception at a restaurant about two feet away. That is absolutely the way to have a wedding. No driving from the church to the reception – it was all in one place. We had a marvelous time and it was so fantastic to be able to go to such a fun event and not even think about alcohol. I was 55 and a little over two and a half years sober.

It was also an opportunity to spend some time with my parents. I had made amends to them in 2006 and I was so thrilled that I was able to visit them each Christmas since and that they could experience me sober for a few years at least before they went to Heaven. I was always a bit nervous around my father, as he could be so bossy. Not only did this annoy me, but it was also a perfect mirror of myself, which I didn't recognise at the time.

Sadly, my dear dad passed away from heart failure on 14 July 2009 aged 92. He had been married to mum for 62 years and two days. I loved my dad and I really miss him even though he ordered me around all my life. It's funny recalling this, as all my life I have ordered people around too. When I finally realised that, I started doing everything I could to break this ingrained habit. The other thing I did was give unasked for advice to people – all the frigging time. And not only that, I was always very insistent that people should take my advice. Oh dear! That is even harder to pull myself up on, so I am forever a work in progress.

In May 2010, I moved to Blackburn, Victoria. I still remember the day I moved in. I went out to the letterbox, as I'd had my mail re-directed a few days before leaving my previous address. The five letterboxes for the units at this address were all in a block of brickwork at the edge of the drive. An old man was standing at the back of the boxes facing the street and I said hello as I bent down at the front of the boxes to see if I had any mail. The old man said gruffly, "there is only mail in there for Lesley Thomas." I stood up and said, "well, that's me, I've just moved in." He then angrily said to me, pointing back down towards my garage and rubbish bins, "and those bins don't go there." OMG! What happened to "welcome!"

I couldn't believe it. Here was another man in my life ordering me around. It's funny how we get reminders about ourselves until we don't need the lesson anymore. He was another perfect mirror for me, although again, it took me a while to realise that.

The street I moved to was a long tree-lined street with the huge tree canopy meeting in the middle most of the way down. One quiet Autumn Saturday morning I was on my way home in my car and I had just turned into the street at one end and I was struck by what I saw. The tree leaves colours ranged every colour of Autumn from deep burnt red through to bright red, green, yellow, orange, and brown. Some leaves were falling, some trees had already lost half their leaves and the sun (and blue sky) was shining and filtering through all the spaces. Some streaks of sunshine reached to the ground and looked like beams of light from Heaven. It was absolutely stunning and I caught my breath.

I had slowed my car to a crawl the moment I turned into the street. I could hardly believe the beauty of it all. I was amazed by the colours and the incredible shining light that gave the whole scene an ethereal appearance. It was completely magical and I found myself leaning right forward over my steering wheel to take in as much as I could. It was also unusually quiet, as my car was the only one in this normally busy street. I remember thinking, "Oh God, this is so, so incredible, thank you so much."

Suddenly, an odd and loud tapping sound to my left interrupted my thoughts and brought me back to the car. Tap, tap, tap, tap. I looked to my left and saw a man walking down the street on the footpath with his white cane tapping to the left, then the right, so that he could stay on the path. He was blind and completely oblivious to the scene; he was not experiencing the awe of it at all.

My immediate reaction was "oh my God, he can't see this" and I felt incredibly humbled and the most overwhelming gratitude filled me that I could see it. I can't ever remember being so grateful for my eyesight and I felt deeply ashamed for ever being ungrateful for anything in my life. As long as I have my eyesight and my legs to get me around, I am wealthy beyond imagination.

My father didn't believe in God and he didn't believe there was life after death. He often stated there was just nothing after death.

I talked out loud to him a lot after he passed away. The first thing I said to him was that I bet he was surprised to find there is a God after all and that there is life after death. I have to admit, I had a good laugh to myself about that. Then I told him everything that I loved about him and everything that had upset me about him. For the first time, I wasn't scared to tell him how I truly felt because I knew he couldn't answer. I also felt much better about our relationship somehow.

One thing about dad, he could never tell us kids that he loved us directly to our faces. I completely understood that this was because of his own upbringing, but I always wanted him to tell me. When I had to say goodbye to him in a Perth hospital a few days before he passed away I told him that I knew that he loved me and that I loved him too. He didn't say anything, but I felt his discomfort. Any mention of feelings and dad would just shut down. I just couldn't let him go without saying it though.

Several years later, in 2013, I was on a ship attending a Life Journeys, Inc. seminar while sailing up the east coast of Australia. I hadn't planned on going on this trip, but when friends told me the speakers were James Van Praagh (famous medium from the USA) and Mavis Pattilla (famous medium from the UK), my first thought was "maybe I could speak to dad through them," so I booked.

I remember sitting in a seat about two thirds of the way back from the front in a small theatre type area on the ship, where 100 of us attending the seminar were waiting. An American medium, Karen Glass, who I had never met before came and sat next to me. The first thing she said to me was, "your father is here." I was gobsmacked and desperately wanted to ask her if he said he loved me but didn't ask because I thought she might say "yes," just to be nice.

When James and Mavis came on stage they announced they were going to choose a spirit in the room to talk to, as apparently everyone seemed to have a spirit with them. They looked around the room and chose the girl on my left, then said no, that it was me. James said that I had an elderly gentleman standing behind me wearing a walking hat and who was frantically waving his wooden walking stick at James to get his attention and was calling out loudly, "tell her I love her, tell her I love her."

I was so overwhelmed with emotion. I could almost see dad doing that. He always wore his walking hat and walked with his wooden walking stick. Someone shoved a microphone in my hand and I babbled out the story to them and got all choked up about it and at one point I could hardly speak. My voice was full of tears. That was an "irrefutable evidence of life after death" moment for me and I was so incredibly grateful that my dad loved me enough to go to so much trouble to tell me so. That wasn't the only time my father has visited me since his passing, but it was the most dramatic and most significant.

* * *

In AA, the older sober members say it takes five years for the fog to lift.

In 2010, when I had moved to Blackburn, I was four years sober and had completely missed the most important message in AA.

Added to this, I had struggled with weight issues my whole adult life and had no idea what the real problem about that was at the time.

I had worked to provide for my children and when they left home, for myself, but I didn't have a career as such. I worked because I had to and sometimes it was incredibly depressing and stressful.

My counselor told me that childhood trauma can lead to an adulthood spent in survival mode and that was me to a tee. I was just surviving and I wanted to shift to thriving, but for me, that was excruciatingly slow. Mainly because I had absolutely no idea how to achieve that, nor which direction to move in.

As 2011 came in, I was about to find out what important message I had completely missed in AA and I was also to start getting an understanding of what was going on for me with my up and down weight issues.

And I was soon to become aware of the Angels that are around me in my life.

CHAPTER NINE

Going Beyond Time

Time has always been a big issue for me, but there are several different sorts of time.

Being on time for an appointment sort of time.

Someone being late for dinner sort of time.

People wasting my time.

Possessiveness and selfishness of my time sort of time.

And then there is time that is not a matter of duration. It is the Now, this moment, and this is the most wonderful time to be in. When I am in the Now, I am aware of and alert to an awareness inside of me as well as everything going on around me. I am not thinking and I am not worrying. I am sensing and it's almost like there is no time in that space.

I learned about this sort of time from Eckhart Tolle in his book *The Power of Now*, which I first started reading in 2004. At the time, I read and reread this book for well over a year, as I wanted to ingrain his teachings into my subconscious.

My dad had an issue with time too and I'm sure I developed this trait from constantly seeing him become agitated by things to do with time. Us kids not being immediately obedient, people being late, etc. Being a lieutenant in the navy in the war, he was an absolute stickler for time, so I could fully understand where he got it from. I gave him a copy of *The Power of Now* a few years before he passed away hoping that he might read it, but when I asked him about it once he said he couldn't understand it and after he died I found it unopened on his bookshelf. And that was ok. A person can only hear a truth or a lesson when they are ready and open to it.

I used to think that people's lateness was a direct insult to me and reflected not only what they thought of me, but also my worth as a human. But that's not right at all. If someone is late, it is a reflection of their feelings and beliefs about themselves. It has nothing to do with me at all. If they also show me that they don't value me, my time, or something I've done or made, then that too is not a reflection of me, it just shows me their attention is elsewhere or their values are different and that's absolutely ok. I just then need to make sure that I let it go completely, allow the other person to be who they are, and then I simply don't put myself in the same situation again by repeating my part.

But the one "time" that has caused me big problems, particularly in early sobriety, was my possessiveness and selfishness of my personal time. When I was a child, it was when I was home from school, having afternoon tea and watching TV or any free time I had on the weekend away from my father's strictness. As an adult, it was any time after work finished. Usually, that was evenings and weekends. Because of the childhood belief system of my role in life to be a wife, mother, and homemaker and my seeming inability to carve out some sort of purposeful career for myself, any employment positions I had were mainly just a means to an end, rather than something I was passionate about. I always made sure I did my best in any role I undertook, but if money was not an issue, I wouldn't have been there.

So, after I had spent all day at work, I found I was very reluctant to talk to anyone at night. Plus (and I am almost ashamed to admit it, but I will), there was not a lot I enjoyed more than eating some scrumptious comfort food while watching a great show or movie on TV. I didn't have to think. I could relax. There was no pressure on me to be or do anything. Back in those days I was also drinking and smoking too, so I was fully into escapism and in escapism, there is no time at all.

Unfortunately, the possessiveness and selfishness of my time coupled with my intense fear of new people getting close to me in case I was triggered (and either frightening, annoying, intimidating, or offending them), really affected my early recovery in AA. It was the base cause for me missing the most important aspect of the program for a long time and stunting my progress enormously.

Part of the 12th step in recovery is to pass on the message to others still suffering from the disease of addiction by talking to the newcomer at meetings and sponsoring others through the program. During the first few years of my recovery, I only sponsored one person. And I couldn't understand why I felt so unhappy. A saying in AA is that you have to give it away to keep it. I had no idea that what we give to someone else is strengthened in ourselves, but I knew I had a problem, so set about finding myself a new sponsor.

2011 was both difficult and exciting, in several ways. Firstly, I had to re-do the A A 12 Step recovery program with a new sponsor. My sponsor was gorgeous, but the work was challenging and very difficult at times.

Secondly, I still had huge problems with my weight going up and down according to what was happening or not happening in my life and how I was feeling at the time. Over the previous 40 years, I had tried every diet known to man: some worked, some didn't. By 2011, I was still fairly clueless about my food intake and had been in a routine for several years of having meal replacement shakes for breakfast and lunch during the week at work and a chicken salad for dinner to counteract the weekends when I would eat whatever I wanted and mostly binged. It was a disastrous way to eat and I thought my mental state and my lack of direction and purpose were the main cause, but I also felt powerless to change that because I had tried so many different courses and workshops over the years that I had lost hope that I would find a career I loved. It was a vicious cycle and I hadn't even realised at that stage that I was addicted to certain foods.

Added to that, the branch of the company I worked for was moved under the control of another section of the company, which was run by Maverick (not his real name) the micro-manager from planet Zorton and his controlling manager Carter (not his real name). Truly, my immediate manager and I nearly went insane trying to please these two people and many, many times would just end up in tears. Literally. We could not believe the way they treated us. Thinking of the mirror though, I remember thinking even back then that I knew I could never be a manager, as I knew I would micro-manage other people myself if I was. That gave me some understanding of Maverick and made it easier to forgive him. And I wanted to forgive him. One of the most important things I've learned in the AA program is that holding on to a resentment is like taking poison and expecting the other person to die.

A night of wonderful relief came on 11 May 2011, when I went to an Andre Rieu concert in Melbourne. The reunited Seekers were to be his support act and, as I had never been to one of their concerts growing up, that was added incentive. On top of that, I had splashed out and bought a VIP ticket, which I was just so excited about. This involved arriving at 4 pm and watching the sound rehearsals for both Andre, the orchestra, and the Seekers. Then at about 5:30 pm our group was taken up to a special dining area and were served the most scrumptiously delicious meal, where some of Andre's orchestra joined us for a chat. After dinner, we were taken down to our reserved seats in the first three rows, my seat being in the first row. I was absolutely thrilled to bits. The show was incredible and I will be forever grateful for being able to attend. After the show, we were taken backstage to have individual photos taken with Andre (which were printed and signed by Andre that night) and also to join him and the orchestra for supper. It was a truly amazing night and one I will never forget. Extravagant yes, but I will have the memory forever; to me, that is priceless, along with the experience of it, which is far more valuable than material things.

Halfway through the year I was about ready to shoot myself at work when I got an email from Hay House Australia advising about a 13 night Islands of the Pacific Seminar Cruise in January 2012, which was being organised by Life Journeys, Inc. from the USA, with Dr. Wayne Dyer as the seminar speaker. I still remember the moment I read about it. My soul leaped and I felt ignited on the inside. I also became aware of my father and felt he was telling me from the spirit world that I should go. However, I was immediately dumped down to Earth again once I looked at what it would cost. My heart sank.

Then a month later, I received the biggest tax return I had ever received. I was so shocked that I just stared at it for ages. My immediate thought was that dad was helping me pay for it. I could now afford to go on the cruise, so I booked it, right then and there. This gave me a huge incentive to not only lose the 10-15 kilos I had put on again in the first half of the year, but it also kept me going until the end of the year. I was so stressed and depressed at work, but just focused on this trip and clawed my way through the months. My manager did the same. She booked a fantastic trip with her husband and children to Paris and just hung on to that. We both decided that once we were back in the new year, we would each look for a new job. So, in the second half of 2011, we had a plan and a holiday to be excited about.

2011 brought home to me the importance of having something to look forward to. Up until that point in my life, I could count on my left hand the number of overseas holidays I'd had in the previous 40 years. I didn't count the occasional trip to Perth since I'd left in 1995 to see family and friends as a holiday; to me they were a break from the grind, albeit a lovely break.

I received some criticism for booking Andre Rieu and the seminar cruise, as neither was cheap. It was suggested to me that I should be saving that money for my retirement years. This unasked-for advice really annoyed me. Actually, it upset me enormously. How anyone who hadn't walked in my shoes could possibly understand how desperately I needed relief from the ongoing shit in my life didn't register though. I was to come to understand over the years ahead that everyone has a different level. One person's worst nightmare is almost normal for the next person and yet an unbelievable horror for someone else. And no-one on planet Earth can understand another person's pain without having experienced it for themselves. One can only imagine it.

Even though the work year was the worst I've ever experienced in my entire life, I was given another gift to brighten that year. A second very dear school friend was to be married in Perth in December 2011. So now I had two trips to be over the moon about. Perth in December for the wedding and to see my mother, family, and friends, then the seminar cruise in January 2012. I could hardly believe my good fortune. Every day I thanked God for such wonderful things to look forward to. I had never wanted to go on a cruise again after I won the trip on the Russian ship from the 13th century when I was 22, but from the photos, this Holland American ship, although half the size of other ships in that fleet, looked fantastic. Plus, there were 500 like-minded people from all over the world coming to Australia to board the ship in Sydney and attend the seminar. I was sure it was going to be an awesome trip.

And it was. I still remember boarding. I was halfway across the gangplank and I stopped to make a memory. At that moment, no one else was on the gangplank. I could hardly believe this trip was really happening for me. I was incredibly excited, incredibly thankful, and incredibly joyful and I have held the memory of that wonderful moment to this day.

Seminar cruising is absolutely the only way to cruise. Not only do you have an event to attend, you instantly have access to like-minded people. You don't have to spend days trying to find like-minded people amongst all the people on board; they are all there instantly on the first day. Also, it was ideal for me because I was traveling alone, but I was still part of something big that was happening on board, so I still felt connected to other people. I also had my own room that I could retreat to if I needed to have some space for a while. Best of all, I only had to unpack once. It was perfect for me.

The seminar started with a private meet and greet type of event on the first evening, so we were straight into the fun as we were leaving Sydney Harbour. All of the seminar times were held on days we were at sea, then when we landed in a port somewhere, groups of us that had been drawn together would get off the ship and explore or relax on a beach somewhere.

We also had a cocktail party halfway through where we got to meet and chat with Dr. Wayne Dyer. One of the things he said during the seminar that stuck in my mind was "if you knew who walked beside you, you would never feel alone again." I have never forgotten that.

There was a second event happening on this trip. Doreen Virtue was running an Angels Workshop, which was also organised by Life Journeys, Inc. Although I only attended the Dr. Wayne Dyer event, I was interested in Angels. I wasn't completely sure if I really believed in them at that stage or not, but I had purchased one of Doreen's Angel Card decks many years earlier and used to give myself readings.

The ship and everything about the trip were spectacular to me. The event, the islands we visited, the yummy food, the people I met. All were absolutely awesome. I am still so very grateful for that trip and have fabulous memories of a truly hilarious time with the group that I was a part of. And we are talking serious pain in the tummy, belly laughing here. Every day was glorious fun. And Dr. Wayne Dyer's teachings were truly insightful.

In late January 2012 I went back to work. Clunk. My manager and I were surprised to learn that the Head Office was going to put our branch back the way it was on or about mid-2012. We decided we could grit our teeth and cope with Maverick until then, but after a couple of months, Maverick was asked to leave. In a quiet moment to myself, I did feel for him, as he appeared to be triggered in a similar way that I was and he had upset a lot of people just like I had in the past. I felt compassion for him but was not sorry he had left.

My manager and I were greatly relieved actually and felt like a huge weight had been taken off our shoulders. I ended up doing so well that year that at the awards night, I won a gold Oscar look-alike statue for best sales in my category Australia-wide. I was stunned, to be honest. It was a huge company and winning something like that wasn't possible in my mind.

I also continued working with my new AA sponsor in 2012, but at one point she told me that my dream of meeting a wonderful man and remarrying was a pipe dream and that I needed to get real, do something about trying to buy my own home and provide my financial security for retirement. I was 58. She might as well have just kicked me in the teeth and knocked my head off at the time. My childhood understanding and beliefs of my life were being smashed to pieces and I reacted very badly and told her I couldn't work with her anymore.

It was a few years before I came to realise that she was right. Not only that, I wanted it for myself. I didn't want to be dependent on a man for anything like my mother had been. To completely change my thinking on this drummed-in childhood belief was quite staggering for me, even if it did take me so long. A huge bonus was that my sponsor back then and I came together again in friendship several years after my blow up and we have enjoyed a very special friendship ever since. I love her to bits and I treasure her friendship.

Digressing in time a little, back in March 2012, I was early for a movie, so popped into a bookstore and a book jumped off the shelf at me. I was immediately drawn to it. It was *Angels in My Hair* by Lorna Byrne. I remember asking myself if I believed in Angels and I thought yes I did, so I bought it.

This was one of two books I have read in my life that I absolutely could not put down. As soon as I started reading it, I immediately knew I was reading the truth. I could feel it in my body and I was absolutely enthralled by Lorna's life and experience with Angels and Spirits. Lorna was the same age as me and had grown up in Ireland and had seen and talked with Angels since birth. It was a truly amazing story and when I finished it, I bought everything else she had written, several more decks of Angels Cards, and my passion for connecting to Angels and doing Angel Card readings was ignited.

It would not be long before I was to have some truly amazing experiences with Angels, Fairies, Orbs, and Spirits and also discover some life secrets that would bring to me much greater wellbeing in every area of my life, especially my eating and weight issues.

CHAPTER TEN

Angels, Spirits, Fairies, and Orbs

A cceptance is a gift to treasure.

The biggest frustration for me in my recovery from traumas, addictions, weight issues, and getting away from and over the nightmare relationship I had in my early 40s was that I found it exceedingly difficult to maintain my morning and evening peace during the day at work because of the human factor. I would start the day having a deep sense of being connected to the spirit in me, then as the day's frustrations commenced at work, be plummeted straight into a stressed-out egoic state.

I was also completely alone, or so I thought. I did not have a human partner to run things past, be comforted by, get a hug from, etc.

That is not a whinge: it's simply a statement on how it was and is. This aloneness was always compounded on a Sunday afternoon when a weird sort of uncomfortable and inexplicable distress and sense of pointlessness would come over me. It was truly awful and was only relieved by binging on comfort food and comfort TV watching when I would stop thinking and feeling.

However, the morning and evening peace slowly grew with the growing awareness of a power greater than me and the Angels and Spirits around me. Also, in AA I learned about acceptance. Acceptance of who I was and where I was at and complete acceptance that the beings around me really were there and were helping me. There have been far too many miraculous and amazing occurrences for me to doubt it for a moment.

There is a really beautiful prayer in AA about acceptance, which starts by stating that acceptance is the answer to all my problems today and that is so true for me.

The prayer goes on to talk about how the only reason I am disturbed is because I find some person, place, thing, or situation unacceptable to me. How simple it is to just allow myself to accept whatever is happening and offer no resistance at all and to just trust that something way more powerful than me had a hand on things. How freeing.

When I stopped to consider the simplicity and truth in that, it really helped me to be much more aware of what was happening for me on the inside when anything came up that I would normally not want to accept.

Further on in the prayer, it says that the only way I could experience any serenity would be if I accepted that person, place, thing, or situation as being exactly the way it is supposed to be. After all, who am I to demand anyone or anything to not be the way it is supposed to be? What right did I have to judge anyone or anything? Who did I think I was? God?

The most significant part of the prayer is at the end where it says that I need to concentrate not so much on what needs to be changed in the world (or others), but on what needs to be changed in me and my attitudes. Bingo! Jackpot! Ring-a-ding-ding! Hooley frigging dooley, that is gold!

It made me think of my nightmare relationship and how I used to think if only he was more like this or if only he would do that. That's not unconditional love. That's control. He was a great mirror and slowly became less of a nightmare and more of a teacher of what needed to be changed in me as time went on.

I turned 60 in 2013 and officially became an old crone! Something I was quite happy and slightly amused to accept. That year also marked another turning point for me. It was around this time that I found another sponsor and re-did the 12 Steps in AA again. It was really important to me to keep working on myself, especially as I still had my trigger, still had food issues, and was still dealing with the mental side of the disease, so I was happy to re-do the program along with other healing programs outside of AA that I was doing at the time. Plus, a couple of girls asked me to sponsor them around this time, which helped my recovery enormously and hopefully theirs too.

In an earlier chapter, I talked about the unexpected cruise that I went on in 2013 in the hopes of talking to my father in the spirit world. That was a truly amazing trip and my father's appearance was nothing short of miraculous to me. A real gift that I will always treasure.

In 2014, I attended a Doreen Virtue Angel Card Reading Workshop in Melbourne and became a certified Angel Card reader. I love doing Angel Card readings for people. It is quite amazing what happens. I found that I never had to actually deal cards. While I shuffled and talked to both our Guardian Angels about what the person needed to know or asked for an answer to a question, cards would just fly out. The amazing thing was that every time this happened, the cards were completely relevant to that person's life. I never ceased to be amazed by this, even to this day.

Around this time, I thought I'd take a break from my life and try online dating again. After scrolling through profiles of men with photos of themselves posing with either wild animals or with a huge motorbike or bare-chested on horseback or flying through the jungly tendrils half-naked, I found a really lovely man who was looking for a woman of about the same age. As I mentioned in an earlier chapter, this was rare, as most men my age seemed to be looking for women a lot younger when I tried online dating a few years earlier.

We met and we spent a lot longer than my standard half hour maximum over our coffee. He suggested a walk around the local lake through the bushland so that we could continue chatting, so I agreed. After walking a while we sat on a park bench and I asked him why he had gone onto this particular dating site. I didn't tell him that I just couldn't understand why a gorgeous man like him didn't have a line of women wanting to date him.

Without drawing breath, he replied, "well, I was talking to a friend of mine and telling him about how owning my own real estate business meant I had to work all weekend and nights and that I live on this really big property that I have to use a ride-on mower to mow and it takes about an hour and a half, plus my 17-year-old son who doesn't drive is living with me and needs to be run around for footy training and lots of other things and my 26-year-old daughter who has mental issues has come home to live and needs attention and my friend said: mate, you need a wife, so I came online and found you."

After picking my jaw up from the gravel path and spitting out a fly, I said to him that I was at a time of my life where I wanted things to be easier, not harder and that while I was perfectly willing to take on the effort required to make a relationship work and would be willing to give the ride-on mower a bit of a whirl and help with the kids where I could, I was not looking for a relationship where my partner was going to be out at night and away on weekends. I suggested he hire a gardener and a housekeeper. He was genuinely perplexed, which absolutely astounded me. He just couldn't believe I was knocking him back. In fact, he kept ringing me to ask me out for dinner and I just kept telling him no. To me, it was a complete waste of time spending any further time with him. In the end, I told him I'd go out for dinner with him when he had retired from real estate, sold his business, and preferably when his kids had left home and he had sold his property and ride-on mower and was ready to enjoy life. I never heard from him again.

After that experience, I never tried online dating again. I realised I must still be looking for a man for the wrong reasons just like that man had done in what he wanted a woman for. A crystal clear mirror he was. I noticed that I kept getting the same lessons until I learned what it was that I needed to learn. Once I realised and accepted something, I never had to repeat that lesson again. So, slowly but surely, I was moving forward.

Christmas 2014, I went to Perth to visit my darling mum. She was 88 and had vascular dementia and Alzheimer's and a year or so earlier, my brothers and I had had to make the hard decision and organise for her to move into a nursing home in Perth. I visited as often as I could, but it was really hard seeing her like that. I was greatly comforted though from what medium Mavis Pattilla said about people with dementia and Alzheimer's during the 2013 cruise when my father had appeared. She said that people with these diseases spend 75% of their time in the spirit world. The amazing medium from the USA, Karen Glass, who attended that seminar and was the girl who had first told me of my father's presence the day we met, also mentioned a couple of times during that trip that my mum was there with my dad. One day, we were sitting by the pool and she said that mum and dad were there, they were young, about the age when they married and were chasing each other around the pool, laughing and having a wonderful time. That news really warmed my heart.

On 16 February 2015, I was outside hand-watering my plants after work. While watering my African violets, thoughts of mum filled me, memories flooded in and I started to cry – almost uncontrollably. I couldn't get over how upset I was and I found myself asking her out loud if she would visit me when she passed away and telling her how much I loved her and apologising for all the things I didn't do or should have done in my life. It was such a weird experience and nothing like it had ever happened before.

Exactly 15 minutes later, as I walked back inside, the phone rang. It was my older brother ringing from Perth. He said, "mum passed away 15 minutes ago, I was with her." I knew then that mum had just been to see me. I was completely in awe of what I had just experienced in the garden with her. I was deeply touched and felt so blessed that she had come to see me so quickly after passing.

The next day I stayed home from work and I wanted some time alone with my thoughts of mum. However, due to a very demanding job, I was on my home computer sorting urgent problems all day. At 5:30 pm a psychic medium friend rang me and said, "your mother has been trying to talk with you all day. She's so happy because she can remember 'this' and remember 'that.' She is literally dancing for joy and she wants you to stop working (my friend did not know I was working), make a cup of tea and go outside into your courtyard and be with her right now." I dropped what I was doing immediately.

In a chair outside with my cup of tea, I felt extremely emotional. I talked to my mum about things I wasn't proud of in my life and again felt a need to apologise to her. Then I heard her voice and she said: "Dizzy Lizzy (her nickname for me that she had not used for many years), there is nothing to forgive. I love you darling. It's beautiful here, your dad is with me and I am so happy." I can't even begin to express the immense comfort that filled my heart in those moments.

Since then, I have often felt the presence of both mum and dad and it has been an enormous comfort to me. I needed it at the time, as it was an extremely stressful year at work. Luckily though, I was also super inspired that year, as early the previous year I had booked a fantastic seminar cruise for September 2015. Ibis Kaba, Executive VP/Producer for Life Journeys, Inc. had organised an incredible trip: a "Wayne Dyer 14 days of Self Discovery – Holy Land and Beyond" seminar cruise from Rome to Jerusalem, Nazareth and Galilee which also included stopping in Naples on the way to Jerusalem and Ephesus, Mykonos, Athens and Valletta on the way back to Rome. Also speaking on this cruise was Anita Moorjani, who came back to life after being in a coma with final stage cancer and having the most amazing near-death experience I have ever heard, and Immaculee Ilibagiza, who had survived the 1994 Rwanda genocide, which claimed most of her family. Booking that trip in early 2014 kept me going for 18 months.

Before I went on the cruise I went to the UK to visit my son who had been living and working in London for several years. It was so fantastic seeing him again and we went on a country driving adventure together. I had researched the little country villages where Midsomer Murders was filmed and found there was a northern trail and a southern trail, so we did the northern trail of villages the first day and stayed overnight in a 15th-century pub, then did the southern trail the next day before driving on to Bath. I thoroughly enjoyed this time with my son and exploring a part of the UK countryside. Bath was a stunning spot and we stayed overnight then drove down to Stonehenge the next day before heading back to London.

Something else rather special happened on that trip with my son. We had stopped by a grass and woodland tree area situated by running water. It was such a beautiful little spot and we got out of the car and sat near the water for a while. At one point, I was gazing into the tall grasses and shrubs under some woodland trees and I swear black and blue that I saw a fairy. I just stared at it as it moved and then flew away. It reminded me of a wonderful movie I have at home called *Fairy Tale, A True Story* starring Peter O'Toole. And it is a true story. In 1917, two English girls photographed fairies in the garden. The photos were authenticated images, with no trace of trickery. It's a great little film and I certainly believe in fairies.

I had also contacted one of my favourite authors Sue Stone (author of *Love Life, Live Life*, and *The Power Within You Now*) a few months beforehand and asked if I could take her out for lunch while I was in the UK. Much to my delight, she accepted and we had a wonderful time. Sue is a truly amazing woman, full of life and full of self-motivation, and has an incredibly inspiring story. I felt so honoured to have that time with her.

My cruise was to be the trip of a lifetime, but sadly Dr. Wayne Dyer passed away a month before we were due to sail. As it was way too late to cancel anything, and Robert Holden, author of ten best-selling books was fortunately available, he agreed to join us as a speaker to replace Wayne. Robert is a happiness guru and was a wonderful and uplifting speaker. It was so good of him to join us at such short notice.

A truly amazing thing happened when we got to Jerusalem. Orbs started appearing in my photos when I went into ancient religious buildings. I was told these free-flowing transparent balls were spirits. When we got to Galilee, Life Journeys, Inc. had organised a special dinner and evening's entertainment at a private home out in the desert somewhere. There were 500 of us for dinner. It was a fantastic night and every photo I took had literally thousands upon thousands of orbs of all sizes in them. It was breathtaking. I also got someone to take a photo of me with a camel that was sitting down near all our tables and I could hardly believe the orbs around me in that photo as well. It was a phenomenal sight. Once we left the holy land, the orbs in photos stopped, so I knew it wasn't my iPhone camera.

At one point on that trip, we were to pass Crete. My dad's ship in the war, *Fiji*, was sunk near Crete and before the trip, my older brother had given me a map of where it had gone down. I spoke to someone in authority on our ship and he said that we wouldn't be passing that spot until sometime after midnight very early the next morning and he couldn't give me an exact time. When I went to bed that night, I doubted I would be able to get up at the right time, especially as I had no idea when that might be, so there was no point setting an alarm. I asked my Guardian Angel to wake me up at the right time. At 2 am in the morning, I was woken by my dad and he said that we were about to pass the spot where his ship went down. I immediately sprung out of bed and went out onto the balcony and shared a really special little while with him.

107

As I stood there on the balcony that night, looking out into the darkness and watching the wake from our ship, I could hardly imagine how frightening it must have been to have been in that shark-infested water in the middle of the night not knowing if or when you would be rescued.

It made me feel extremely grateful for everyone and everything I had in my life and that my country was not at war. I was also exceedingly grateful to have had such a wonderful trip as that one to plan for and look forward to for so long beforehand and then to enjoy and have the memories of forever.

Gratitude helped me put more into perspective my own struggle, particularly at that point with my food issues. There was a solution and I was continually working towards healing. I had discovered a few years after getting sober that I was addicted to processed sugar and processed flour, both of which triggered overeating once I had these substances in my system.

As time went on, I also discovered that I was addicted to diet Coke, sugar-free lollies, Vicks Vapodrops, and chocolate protein bars. As ludicrous as that sounds, it was true for me. These products nearly sent me into overdrive and it was only having something to look forward to that helped me manage the intense cravings because I did not want to go on a trip looking like a cookie monster. So, vanity spurred me on to diet and not overeat. However, it was a huge struggle for me, especially on the weekends when that enormous unease I mentioned earlier would come over me, and all I could think of doing to relieve it was binge comfort eat and watch TV. Plus, I still wasn't eating properly during the week in general. It wouldn't be until 2016 that I would strike gold in that area.

CHAPTER ELEVEN

The Magic Bullet

Forgiveness is the most beautiful gift a person can give to another, but more importantly, to themselves.

Forgiveness doesn't mean what the other person said or did to me was ok, it just simply means I don't want to carry anger around in my heart and in my body because of what someone else has said or done. To top that off, while I hold on to a grievance and go over it again and again in my mind, the only person I am harming is me. More often than not, the other person has not given me another thought. The other thing about forgiveness is that if I won't forgive, then I must be judging because I have to justify why I won't forgive.

So, why on Earth would I want to waste my precious time on a grievance and why on Earth would I want to harm my own body and mind? I choose instead to be absolutely beautiful to me and to give myself all the love and comfort I could possibly need.

Every now and again something will happen that will cause my ego to immediately be annoyed or feel resentful. Straight away I am on my knees telling God that although I can still feel the annoyance in my heart or body, I am willing to let it go and I'm willing to forgive the person and that I would pray about it every day until I felt it released from me. Sometimes, that would just take a day, sometimes weeks, and once or twice in the past a lot longer, but I kept doing it until it was gone. I could only ever be doing all that for me, so the pointlessness of holding onto a grudge really hit home to me.

So, my standard policy is that I always forgive everyone for everything, no matter what they have done and no matter how long it takes. Forgiveness is the goal. Plus, I never base how I behave on how someone else has treated me. For example, I wouldn't not send someone a Christmas card purely because they didn't send me one. If I wanted to send them joy in a card, I'd just do it and happily.

I am the one who benefits if I choose to forgive people and I am the one who suffers if I don't. And there is tremendous power, relief, joy, and freedom that comes upon me as I just let things go and forgive.

There are other things I do for self-care, but one of the most important was getting help to learn to eat the right foods, exercise, and get as fit as I could for my age. It was something I have always wanted to do and I had a burning desire to be strong, to grow some muscle, and to feel good on the inside.

Over time I noticed that if I ate any foods containing processed sugar and flour, addiction would set in immediately. The disease of addiction is progressive, which means that it is always increasing in the background and if I was to pick up a drink today, it would be far worse for me than the day I stopped. So, processed sugar and flour started to be a really big problem for me and I found that if I comfort ate for the two days over a weekend and then didn't pull myself up on the following Monday and stop, but kept going and had more processed sugar and flour, then what I was eating started to change the way I was thinking and feeling. It was almost like a complete personality change. I found that I didn't want to go back to good food. As weird as that sounds, that's what happened. Then the mental obsession would kick in and eating those substances was all I could think about. And so another battle to get off them would start. It was like a reccurring nightmare. Truly ruly, someone shoot me!

I also tried other things like sugar-free lollies, protein bars, etc, as mentioned in the previous chapter, but became addicted to whatever I ate that wasn't a quality food or that contained an addictive chemical and the whole addiction process would start again. I got an extra sponsor around this time to just spend time reading through the AA Big Book and Steps, as I knew I had to continue to work on the mental side of the disease as long as the physical side was acting out with one substance addiction or another. I also started going to meetings at Overeaters Anonymous (OA) and Al-Anon to support this.

I needed professional health and fitness guidance and I needed to make exercise a habit, a part of my life's routine, something I just did without thinking about it. I didn't want to have a "will I, won't I" argument every day with myself about whether or not I was going to do it. Like when I wake in the morning and need to go to the toilet. I don't just lie in bed and say to myself that I can't be bothered, I'll just do it here in bed. No, I automatically get out of bed without thinking about it and go to the toilet. That's how I wanted my exercising and, ultimately, my eating to be in my life. Automatic.

I also needed to get off meal replacement shakes for breakfast and lunch and I needed accountability. The only thing that ultimately worked for me was hiring a personal trainer to help me achieve all this. Miraculously, within what seemed like moments of this decision at the end of 2016, a personal training studio opened closeby to where I live and I was in there with bells on my toes in January 2017. My trainer, Kimberley Hinschen, met me at the door and I was instantly drawn to her vibrancy and incredibly uplifting and happy nature.

Luckily for me, Kimberley was a Sport and Exercise Scientist and Nutritionist. That's a food specialist. Bingo!

Kimberley set about discovering my weight, fitness, and muscle tone goals along with what food I was currently eating. She then created a program for me with an exercise routine and an eating plan consisting of the number of carbs, proteins, and fats I was to eat each day to achieve my new goals. The training went brilliantly, but I couldn't get my head around the good food plan. To me, it looked like way too much food and I stayed with my meal replacement shakes for breakfast and lunch during the day. I did lose weight, but I lost muscle and gained loose skin because of the way I was eating. There was so much about the types of food to eat and when to eat them that I didn't understand at that point. However, I did keep my exercising routine up and did get fitter.

In June 2017, I was made redundant from my job and the completely bizarre thing about that was that the previous week I had been off sick for about eight working days, which had never happened before. While at home I had really, really slowed down.

I allowed my body to wake up when it was ready, I then got myself a cup of coffee and spent quite a long time just talking to God out loud about everything and anything, like he was a friend in the room. I also prayed and meditated. I sank into a deep peace over those days even though I was unwell. It was just so blissful to be away from the stress of my job. I loved this peacefulness so much that on one of the last days I said to God that if it was up to me, I'd spend time with Him every morning like this, then I'd exercise, and then I'd get on with whatever else I had to do to each day.

Within a week, I was made redundant and I have been doing exactly that every day ever since with very rare exceptions. Redundancy meant that I couldn't financially continue with personal training with Kimberley though. However, I reveled in my new morning routine with my Higher Power and exercising in the local park on my own. Unfortunately, because I had a measure of fear about financial insecurity pounding on my ego self, I went right back into comfort eating and put back on most of the weight I had lost. Again.

I knew this continual up and down of 10-15 kilos over the years was bad for my health and it was also really bad for my skin. When I went back to Perth after finishing school aged 18 and very quickly lost a pile of weight I ended up with stretch marks on my chest and the tops of my legs and they would be with me for life. I didn't learn the importance of gaining and losing weight slowly back then. Probably because no one knew much about it. It was the late 60s at the time.

Fortunately, in March 2018, the volume of online work at home increased substantially, so I went back to see Kimberley. This time I had a different attitude. I was fed up to the back teeth with my yoyo weight and dieting issue and so sick of feeling like crap on the inside that I told her I would eat and do whatever she told me to, that I was surrendering. Surrender is another gift to treasure. It freed me to do what I didn't want to do in order to achieve what I needed to achieve for my own good.

That was the start of a whole new ball game for me. I committed myself to my mental, emotional, physical, spiritual, and financial wellbeing from that moment on and it is the very best gift I could ever have given myself. By the end of 2018, I had lost all the weight I wanted to and I was thrilled that I had grown some muscles. I certainly didn't have the toned body of a 20 year old and still had my stretch marks and cellulite, but I just didn't care about that. After the hammering my body had endured over the years from nicotine, alcohol, and weight yoyoing, I was ecstatic to be feeling so good on the inside and as fit as I could be for my age. Then 65. My cat, however, raised an eyebrow before turning away with the worst look of disgust that I have ever seen on a cat when he saw me naked. I kid you not. I used to be intimidated by this and turn my back on him or go to another room when getting dressed. The expression on his face was like – really? Now, I just have a good laugh about it.

When I went back, Kimberley gave me a bio scan and then helped me re-plan my meals and cardio and weights exercising. She also made sure I was eating the most carbs in the morning and the least at night to maximise the results. It was all calculated out so that I knew exactly where I was and exactly what I had to do to get where I wanted to be. We all have different body shapes and metabolisms and our metabolisms all function differently: some are faster and some are slower. That really brought home the importance of having a qualified food and exercise specialist work out the most effective food and exercise plan for my body and metabolism type, so that I could reach my goals.

At last! An awesome plan that worked brilliantly for me. Unfortunately, when COVID-19 hit Australia in March 2020, I lost my online job, was plummeted into lockdown, and had to stop my training with Kimberley again. As before, I kept up all my exercise on my own at home and in the park and created EXCEL sheets with a new food plan, which Kimberley helped me work out before I left. I should say here that food plans change in accordance with weight loss/gain, muscle loss/gain or changing goals or exercise routines. I have a food plan for my cardio days, one for my strength/weights days and one for my accelerator day and I weigh and measure everything I eat. This works for me and I feel a million dollars on the inside. I am just so ecstatic about it.

Some of the other really important things that I learned when working with Kimberley were not to do cardio exercise for at least two to three hours after eating, otherwise, I'd just be working off the food and not the fat on my body. Also, not to eat for at least an hour after doing cardio exercise for the same reason. It was also important for me to have a protein shake within half an hour of exercising, especially on my strength/weights days, so that my muscles would use the protein in that to replenish and grow. I also learned not to have more than two cups of instant coffee each day because coffee can negatively affect muscle growth, not to eat carb-filled fruit at night, especially an apple, and the faster I lose weight, the more likely I am to put it all back on and end up with loose skin and more stretch marks. Far better to go slowly, but surely. I wish I'd known that when I was 17.

Self-care has become incredibly important to me. I do all sorts of things to nurture my body, mind, and spirit and I love that I do that for me. Once a month, I have a body massage with the most incredible therapist. Every time she gives a massage, it's like the first time. Superb. Absolutely superb. She never becomes complacent – ever. I always look forward to and cherish this heavenly treatment.

Early every morning, I spend time with my Higher Power talking, in prayer and in meditation as the sun comes up. I truly treasure this time with Him. I also always have easy listening music playing in the background for myself, my plants, and the cat that owns me. Usually nature sounds, water, piano, 528 Hz for healing and positivity, etc. It's just peaceful and I love "peaceful."

Willingness has played a big part in my recovery and healing too. Willingness to keep working on myself in AA, with counselors, therapists, and psychologists, etc, and willingness to pick myself up again when I fall down and to be super gentle with myself when that happened.

Amongst other things that I do for self-care are things like eating mindfully and savouring the different tastes and textures of food, especially my breakfast of no-fat Greek yoghurt, natural almonds, fresh strawberries, banana, a few raw oats, and frozen blueberries. I love my blueberries frozen and as soon as I have put them on top, I start eating straight away. It is, without doubt, the most delicious breakfast I have ever had and I savour every mouthful of it every day.

Mostly, I am kind to myself. I also stop and listen to my intuition. I make small realistic changes one at a time. Once I am used to one change, I can move on to the next. I say no if someone asks me to do something that doesn't feel right for me, but I also make myself available for volunteer work. I stopped excluding myself from things and I stopped blaming "me being excluded" on other people's words or actions. I lessen my attention on the world, who said did/what when and to whom, for where I put my attention determines what my experience is going to be. I accept rather than try to change a person, place, situation, or thing and I am immensely grateful for all that I have, especially the little things.

Most importantly, I forgive myself for the harms I've done to others. It took me many, many years to be able to do this. Learning I had a disease and not a moral issue helped enormously. Ultimately though, along with AA, a psychologist explaining that I had PTSD and that the behaviour that followed me being triggered was not who I really was, slowly started the healing.

Amazingly, a magical path and ultimate gifts followed next.

CHAPTER TWELVE

Ultimate Gifts

There is a saying that goes something like, "yesterday is gone, tomorrow is yet to come, today is a gift, that's why they call it the present."

But to "be present" today is the real gift. What does it mean to get or be present? A skier flying down a mountainside is fully present. He isn't thinking about washing his car: he is fully in the thrilling moment, all senses on.

A simple way that I get present is to sit quietly, hands at my side, but not touching my body, close my eyes, and ask myself how do I know that my hands are still there. My attention immediately leaves my head and is transported into my hands. I am not thinking, I am sensing. I am being present at that moment.

I love being in this awareness state. I can most easily get there when I spend time with my Higher Power in the mornings. It is an incredibly alive and alert state, but also a very peaceful one for me. However, as I said earlier, I found it extremely difficult to take this state with me when I went out the front door, especially when getting behind the wheel of a car.

Late 2018, I woke up at 2 am and something made me look on Facebook. An Eckhart Tolle event came up. Eckhart Tolle, also mentioned earlier, lives in the present moment all the time. He is quite amazing and once I got my head around what he was teaching, I was greatly interested. I felt compelled to attend this event, as he was to teach more about how to stay present during the day when faced with life outside the home. However, the cost was quite high. I then noticed I could apply for a scholarship, which I did right then and there, and amazingly, it was approved.

This meant that for the first six months of 2019, I was blessed with endless online live seminars and workshops, as I attended Eckhart's School of Awakening. It was a life-changing experience, which I was extremely grateful for.

Being present also helped me more efficiently send energetic love to people. I had been practising this since I was taught how to do it at a Hay House weekend seminar in Sydney over ten years previously. At the time, I hadn't realised how powerful it was.

Instead of holding on to a negative thought or feeling about another person or situation, I could consciously send that person or situation energetic love from my heart. And whether the person was aware of it or not, they were receiving it. I have seen this demonstrated too many times in my life in the most truly amazing ways for me to ever doubt it was working.

Have you ever wondered why a situation won't heal when you or they have already apologised? It's because one or both of you is still holding, and therefore sending to the other, negative thoughts and feelings about it. You can heal that situation by bombarding that person with energetic love. They will receive it, guaranteed. It really does work.

2019 was full of gifts for me. The gifts of sobriety, the gifts of being willing to forgive others, the gifts of just accepting and offering up love to all situations. The gifts of peace.

In February, my son, who lives in London, proposed to his gorgeous English girlfriend and they set the date for their wedding as 28 September 2019. His dream was to be married at the home of his father William (not his real name) and step-mum Catherine (not her real name) in the French countryside near the northern Spanish border.

A couple of years earlier, William had decided, with the encouragement and support of Catherine, to forgive me for my past harms to him when we were married in our 20s. This extraordinary gift of forgiveness brought our family closer together than I had ever thought possible and from then on, whenever William and Catherine came to Australia, we would all go out as a family. It was incredibly healing for each of us and enormously generous of William and Catherine.

Now, I was invited to their home in France to attend our son's wedding. What an incredible gift. We all had a wonderful time planning and William and Catherine worked tirelessly on getting their home and grounds ready for the big day and all the guests. There is a gorgeous clearing surrounded by tall woodland trees where water runs through at the bottom of their property. This was where the wedding ceremony was to be held. It was an incredibly picturesque setting. Back up near the house, a large marquee was set up for the reception.

The local village also got involved and loaned all the village's Christmas fairy lights to decorate the trees and garden from the marquee and house all the way down to and around the area where the ceremony was being held. It was a truly magical sight.

We all arrived in France a week before the wedding. My daughter and I stayed in Biarritz and drove to their home most days and helped with the preparations. Catherine's two daughters joined us as well as my son's fiancé's parents from the UK. It truly was the most incredibly happy and special time leading up to the big day. I felt so blessed to be a part of it all, especially when we were all sitting around the same table enjoying a meal together and laughing together.

The wedding itself was, without a doubt, the most joyful event I have ever been to. It was like every single person that attended was chock-a-block full of joy, love, laughter, and happiness. To top it off, the weather could not possibly have been more perfect. I still can't quite believe how incredible it all was. Nor how lucky we were that they didn't plan the wedding for 2020 in the middle of COVID-19.

Another wonderful gift in 2019 that I was blessed with was being able to attend a Lorna Byrne (author of *Angels in My Hair*) event in Switzerland after the wedding. The timing was amazing and I certainly felt like I had been given an extra gift on that trip. I went to an evening with Lorna in Lucerne, then a two-day workshop in Zurich. I have to say that being in the presence of Lorna and the Angels was a magical and special experience. She is an earth

Angel to me, a real and direct connection to the Divine. At the end of each event, Lorna came to each of us that attended and prayed over us, and blessed us individually. It was a deeply moving experience, one I shall never forget.

My daughter gave me a fantastic gift on 18 June 2019. She sent me a link to *A Course in Miracles* explained by Carol Howe. Wow! Some of the language is not easy to understand and Carol is brilliant at explaining the meanings. The Course is a lesson a day for a year and I added this to my Higher Power time in the mornings. It took me longer than a year, but I recently finished it in October 2020. The Course is a truly beautiful gift, inner peace being its goal, and I loved it so much I am re-doing it.

These amazing gifts of sobriety would never have been possible if I had still been drinking.

2020, however, is certainly a year to remember. When COVID-19 struck Australia in March, I lost my casual online job and because of my age, the government popped me onto the old age pension. Dun dun! This put me instantly into an extremely difficult position financially.

However, as time went on, I had to ask myself an important question. "If money was not an option, how would I be feeling right now?" And, to be honest, the first word that came to mind was "relief," closely followed by "peaceful." I had a great online job and I thoroughly enjoyed the people I worked with, but it was also an extremely stressful job and to not be dealing with that stress daily was quite wonderful for me, despite the financial cost.

It just confirmed for me that the greatest gifts of all are inner joy and inner peace and I experienced this every morning and night when I spent time with my Higher Power. Although I still can't keep that internal state up all day long like Eckhart Tolle, my Higher Power is my path to peace, of that I have no doubt.

So many people in the world make decisions based on whether they are going to gain or lose money. I'm quite sure I did subconsciously in the past too. I realised during COVID-19 that I don't do that in my present life. I am so incredibly grateful for that glorious feeling of inner peace and I feel far richer in my life because of it that this has become far more important to me.

COVID-19 certainly has its challenges, especially where I live in Victoria. We are still in lockdown seven months later as I write this and it is exceedingly difficult for people of all ages to find employment, as so many businesses have closed.

Joyless July was the worst month for me though. Everything seemed to be going wrong: I couldn't stay present, I lost my hold on my inner peace, fear plummeted me into egoic panic and I picked up the comfort food on and off for a few weeks during that month. Anything that had processed sugar and flour in it to relieve me of the anguish I experienced changing from inner peace to inner distress and turmoil. I hadn't even noticed the fear creep in, but it sure took hold.

But there was something even worse about Joyless July for me. My son, who is a passionate filmmaker, was permitted by the West Australian and Australian Federal Governments to fly out from London to Perth to direct the filming of his documentary *After The Night* (also called *The Night Caller* for USA and UK), which is about the serial murderer who was terrifying Perth when I was ten that I mentioned in one of the early chapters. Due to COVID-19 restrictions, I couldn't fly to Perth to see him and he couldn't come to Melbourne to see me. I was really sad that he was so close and I could do nothing about it. In the end, I just had to practise what I preach and accept it and let it go. His four-part documentary series commenced on Stan TV on 29 November 2020 in Australia, on Sundance TV in the USA and SKY Crime in the UK on 15 December 2020, and I'm giving out that information purely because I am so very, very proud of him.

Now that I've mentioned more about my son, I will say a little about my daughter. Bel (not her real name) has grown into a beautiful, strong, passionate, and inspiring woman. She has worked diligently on her own recovery over the years (as has my son) and she has achieved tremendous results, as well as putting herself through uni at night while she worked full time to get her qualifications in Family Counselling. She is currently in her final year of her Masters and has also bought herself her first home without any financial help from anyone. I am enormously proud of her too.

Around the end of July, I sensed that August was going to be awesome. And it was.

Several miraculous things happened in August for me, but the most significant was that I happened to see a Facebook post in early August about a book writing workshop on 18 August being run by a gorgeous girl I know and something pinged inside of me. I attended the workshop and immediately knew that I was meant to write a book and that I would start pretty much straight away. All of a sudden I had direction and was filled with an inner ignition that I have never felt before. This was my purpose. I am meant to be telling my story and helping others overcome their own battles. I can show people that it's possible to get away from unhealthy relationships, recover from this horrible disease, stop yoyo dieting, make a plan for fitness and health, and be happy and really live.

That being 67 does not mean a person has one foot in the grave. I feel so incredibly awesome on the inside and am feeling so fit and healthy that I feel like my life is just starting and I can do anything and go anywhere. I can help others achieve this too.

Within no time, I was writing every spare moment and within two months I was finished. The whole way through, I felt like someone else was writing as many things came up that I hadn't thought of or had forgotten about. I almost felt a tiny bit possessed, as I could hardly think about anything else.

During COVID-19, I have also found loads of things to be grateful for. Several months ago, I was speaking to a friend and she was telling me about her sister who has MS, is wheelchair-bound for life, is blind, has no bladder control, and has to be spoon-fed. At that moment, I felt a deep shame for ever having complained about anything in my life. The fact that I can see and I can walk is on top of my gratitude list and when I stopped to think about it, I found so much more to be grateful for.

Things like running water, heating, cooling, fresh food, washing machine, electricity, shower, a bed, a toilet, TV – the list is endless. And I tried to imagine life without these taken for granted gifts, especially visualising myself having to carry a bucket to the local stream for water. OMG! Just imagine if we had to do that. Something thousands of people all over the world have to do every day.

I certainly haven't won all the cash and prizes in my life and I still have times when I struggle with my food issues, but I have all the free things, the things that really matter, and I have stronger tools now to help me manage my food addictions.

Today, because I am sober, I also have a wonderful and loving relationship with each of my children, my son's wife and her family. I enjoy great long-distance chats with William and Catherine in France. I have a fabulous family and lifelong friends in Western Australia, several beautiful friends here in Victoria, and many gorgeous friends around the world that I have met in my travels in sobriety.

And the greatest gift of all is that I have a truly special connection with a deeply loving Higher Power that has guided me to a sober, healthy, and happy outer life and an immensely peaceful inner life. For this, I will be eternally grateful.

I am so excited about the prospect of helping others overcome their difficulties and feel as alive and wonderful as I feel on the inside. I hope the stories in my book have helped to show that anything is possible for anyone that wants it enough and is willing to look at their own stuff. I promise you, if I can do it, anyone can.

About The Author

Growing up in Perth, Western Australia, to parents Una and Ted Thomas, Lesley's childhood had its share of ups, downs and traumas.

Navigating the rollercoaster of life, a series of events led her through some rock-bottom moments, which she, in turn, used as a base to make major changes.

Lesley has spent the past 48 years in the airline, legal, building, insurance, and advertising industries in flight attendant, administration, project management and advertising sales roles.

For the last 25 of those years, Lesley has also been on an extensive, and often extremely challenging, spiritual and personal development journey. Also, she has over 14 years of experience working with women in 12 Step recovery and the disease of addiction.

Sober now since 21 March 2006, Lesley's clean lifestyle has seen her transform into a fit, vibrant 67-year-old woman.

Lesley's own spiritual and personal development has strengthened her highly intuitive and empathic nature, which enhances her work with others as she taps into her past experiences to shine a light on the unspoken.

Her major strength is her exceptional planning and organising ability: she loves getting her teeth into a project and when she felt guided to write her first book, it poured out of her in just two months.

Lesley has two absolutely wonderful adult children, lives in Melbourne, Australia, and is owned by Soli the cat!

Acknowledgements

I would like to thank my gorgeous kids Kelly and Tom and Tom's beautiful wife Alice for their enthusiastic encouragement and support of me in writing this book, but mostly just for loving me.

A huge heartfelt and grateful thank you to: my beautiful lifelong friend Di Smith for all your endless support, love, encouragement and friendship; my brother Geoffrey Thomas and wife Christine for your fantastic encouragement, love and support; Sue Stone (UK Author & Secret Millionaire) for your inspirational encouragement and support; Ibis Kaba (Executive VP/Producer for Life Journeys, Inc.) for your enthusiastic support and encouragement; Chris Hooper (Chris Hooper Promotions) for your wonderful support and kindness; Jacob Norby (USA author) for your generous time and support; dear friends Rod and Lorraine Davies for your love and endless support; Dominica Mirabella for your wonderful love and support; Lucy Brooks for your love, warmth and support; Nat, Stuart and team at Ultimate 48 Author for your tireless help and support; my truly beautiful lifelong friends Jane Watson, Jill Hugall, Gillus Pappas, Shauna Watson, Carol Gowenlock and Judy Parsons for your love, friendship and support; and my gorgeous ISO buddy Erin Tempest for your constant love, support and friendship.

Lastly, I thank my Higher Power for life, love, laughter, joy, Angels, our book and Your immense peace.

LESLEY THOMAS

After turning 50, **Lesley** made a decision to turn her life around and focus on her mental, emotional, physical and spiritual health and wellbeing – and this wasn't a walk in the park!

This involved overcoming her addictions to nicotine, alcohol, processed sugar and co-dependency, developing her connection to a Higher Power, getting physically and mentally fit and feeling brilliant on the inside.

A raw and honest speaker that isn't afraid to talk about the real issues many women are facing in today's world, Lesley is an open book.

Lesley is now motivating women to take back control of their lives and leave their excuses at the door and sharing her own remarkable journey to sobriety and mental and spiritual wellbeing.

Three things Lesley can speak on are:

- Age is just a number/Life is not over after 60

- Living a clean and sober life and being happy about it!

- Weight loss, health and fitness - What I did to get where I am today physically.

FINDING FABULOUS OVER 60

OVERCOMING TRAUMA AND ADDICTION

WEIGHT LOSS THAT FINALLY WORKED

DETACHING FROM A NIGHTMARE RELATIONSHIP

LESLEY THOMAS

"An incredible read! A hugely inspirational story of transformation"
- Sue Stone - UK Author, Secret Millionaire and Inspirational Speaker

To enquire about engaging Lesley to speak at your next event and for pricings and availabilities

Contact: lesleyt88@bigpond.com

133